GLORIOUS PUDS

Mary Berry is the cookery presenter of the Thames Television programme *Afternoon* and the author of several successful cookery books, including the *Complete Book of Freezer Cooking, Colour Book of Freezer Cookery, Popular French Cookery* and *Popular Freezer Cooking*. She is also co-author of the enormously popular *All Colour Cook Book*.

New English Library Books for Cooks
VARIATIONS ON A RECIPE:
Jean Conil and Hugh Williams
VARIATIONS ON A STARTER:
Jean Conil and Hugh Williams
Bruce de Mustchine's ASIAN COOKBOOK
FINE-FLAVOURED FOOD: Henrietta Green
TOP LEVEL COOKERY FOR TWO: Lynda Goetz
THE COMPLETE BOOK OF HOME PRESERVING:
Mary Norwak
GLORIOUS PUDS: Mary Berry

In preparation:
VARIATIONS ON A MAIN COURSE: Jean Conil and
Hugh Williams

GLORIOUS PUDS

MARY BERRY

NEW ENGLISH LIBRARY

First published in Great Britain in 1980 by J.M. Dent
& Sons Ltd

Copyright © Mary Berry 1980

All rights reserved. No part of this publication may be
reproduced or transmitted, in any form or by any
means, without permission of the publishers.

First NEL Paperback Edition October 1981

Conditions of sale: This book is sold subject to the
condition that it shall not, by way of trade or
otherwise, be lent, resold, hired out, or otherwise
circulated without the publisher's prior consent in
any form of binding or cover other than that in which
it is published and without a similar condition
including this condition being imposed on the
subsequent purchaser.

NEL Books are published by
New English Library Limited,
Barnard's Inn, Holborn,
London EC1N 2JR.

Printed in Great Britain by Cox & Wyman, Reading

0 450 05203 6

Contents

Introduction 1

Flans, tarts and pies 7

Traditional winter puddings 25

Pancakes, batters and fritters 47

Soufflés, mousses and omelettes 57

Cheesecakes 73

Meringues and Pavlovas 81

Milk puddings, yogurt and old-fashioned junket 95

Special cream puddings and cheats 105

In praise of fresh fruit 121

On the continental kick and special gâteaux 135

Easy ice creams and sorbets 145

Index 159

I am tremendously indebted to Clare Blunt for her help
and inspiration and for developing and testing recipes.
Two heads are better than one! These recipes have been
well tried on our families and friends – often I have
included their comments.

Introduction

You can't beat the British when it comes to puddings! Don't let anyone ever fool you into thinking anything different. The Danes may have their pastries, the French their gâteaux, the Italians their ice cream and the Germans their strudels, but for sheer mouth-watering variety the British win every time.

Traditional British cooks seem always to have reserved their creative genius for the dessert course. The meat dishes may sometimes be plain, but the puddings are a dream. They can fill you up on a cold winter's day or cool you down in the summer sun. They can be slimming or fattening, depending on your mood. The memory of a good pudding can linger long after the rest of the meal has been forgotten.

I love making puddings and my family, I am glad to say, love eating them. I have really enjoyed preparing this book, sorting out the recipes and deciding what to include so that you will have as wide a choice as possible. Some, of course, are borrowed from abroad, but the majority are British through and through. Many of them are sure to evoke nostalgia for your childhood – children do so appreciate puddings. It always seems a shame that in the rush and turmoil of adult life we so often decide not to bother about dessert, rushing from the table as soon as the main course is over, perhaps snatching an apple as we go, or else preferring to settle for just coffee instead.

Yet, these days, we have more means of saving time and labour than ever before. There were no electric beaters or liquidizers in our grandparents' day, no home freezers to enable dishes to be made in advance. Some puddings, which today can be prepared in a matter of minutes, used to take far longer and cause far more trouble. The modern cook has all the advantages.

Like most cooking, the secret of success lies in planning in advance and using the best ingredients you can obtain. Some dry ingredients are used in a number of different recipes and, provided they will keep, it is always wise to buy more than you need for a particular recipe and store the rest for use another time.

Before looking at the recipes, you may find it useful to read through some general hints on pudding-making. I have found from experience that they can make all the difference between a quite nice pudding and a superlative one!

THE FREEZER

Oh, what a boon this piece of kitchen equipment can be, especially if you have a large family or do a lot of entertaining! There are a number of pudding ingredients which are not stocked in many shops and stores and you may have to make a special trip to a delicatessen or even to London to get them. It saves time – and in the long run money – to buy a large quantity and store them in the freezer.

I am thinking particularly of such items as ground or flaked almonds, hazel nuts, pistachio nuts, dried apricots and whipping cream. With the nuts, I always separate them into small polythene bags, label them and keep them in a large bag in the freezer. Whenever I use a recipe which calls for, say, six hazelnuts, I simply take the bag out and help myself. Nuts will keep beautifully fresh in the freezer for up to two years and storing them saves me many frustrating hours searching the shops for them before a dinner party or special occasion.

Dried apricots tend to lose their colour and wither away if kept in a store cupboard. In the freezer, however, provided they are well wrapped, they remain usable for over a year.

It is now possible to buy whipping cream packed in large granules for freezer storage. You simply tip out the amount required, allow it to thaw and then whip up the cream for mousses, ice creams and decoration. Seasonable fruits, such as blackcurrants and raspberries are particularly good for freezing. They freeze well and retain their shape and flavour, thus enabling you to use them in dishes long after their season is over.

STORING IN THE FREEZER

Many people get worried about the sort of container to use in the freezer, assuming that only foil containers are suitable. The answer is that almost any dish can be put in the freezer, provided that it is made of a suitable material, is not an unsuitable shape and that you do not mind being without it for some time. Suitable materials are toughened glass, oven glass, enamel, metal, pottery, ceramic or toughened china; which gives you a fairly wide choice! Don't use your best cut crystal! On shape, a simple rule of thumb is that the rim of the container should be as wide as, or wider than, the base. In other words, do not use a ceramic casserole with bulging sides – a sort of tulip shape. It tends to crack and break as the food inside it expands and thaws.

Foil dishes are, of course, a great asset, especially for pies and flans, because they can be put straight from the freezer into the oven. Other dishes should be allowed to reach room temperature before going into a hot oven. Another advantage of the foil dish for baking is that, being an excellent conductor of heat, it enables the underside of a double-crust pie to get brown.

If you cannot afford to have a dish locked away in the freezer but it is nevertheless just right for a particular recipe, freeze the food in it, then tip it out, wrap it in polythene and return to the freezer. When you want to serve the food, unwrap the polythene and replace the item in its original container. It helps to loosen the frozen contents – an apple pie, perhaps, or a mousse – if you dip the dish in hot water for a few seconds to allow the outside to thaw a little and then prise the dish free.

For the best results, use puddings from the freezer within three months. From the safety point of view, it will not matter if you leave them longer – years, if you like – but the texture and flavour will be less good. It is also wise to thaw them slowly – in a refrigerator or the larder – ideally overnight.

Remember that a very large dish, such as a mousse for a party, could take as long as twenty-four hours to defrost satisfactorily in the refrigerator.

Before rushing to dump all your efforts into the freezer, however, here is a word of warning. Not all puddings are suitable for freezing. I have given notes on freezing at the beginning of each chapter, so that if you intend to freeze a particular dish check beforehand that it is all right to do so.

SPECIAL FLAVOURS

There are plenty of essences on the market, which come in little bottles and take up hardly any room in the store cupboard. They are very good and extremely useful for the busy cook. But for that extra touch of luxury, it pays to make up and store some specialities of your own.

Vanilla and lemon sugars, for example, are delicious to use. For the former, just store a couple of vanilla pods in a jar of sugar, and use the sugar when making custards, sauces and other recipes. Vanilla pods can be bought at most large chemists. Incidentally, for vanilla-flavoured milk, borrow one of the vanilla pods from the sugar jar and infuse it by placing it in the milk and heating it gently to get the maximum flavour from the pod. Afterwards, remove the pod, wash it in water, dry it thoroughly and return it to the sugar jar. In the recipes that follow, I have specified vanilla essence whenever a vanilla flavouring was required, just in case you had no vanilla sugar. But if you have, always use it in preference to the essence.

Lemon sugar is made in a similar way to vanilla sugar, using grated lemon rind stirred into a jar of sugar instead of the vanilla pods. Because of the moisture in the rind, the sugar may get a little lumpy but this does not matter. Just bang the lumps with the back of a spoon before adding the sugar to the recipe.

Save the grated rind for lemon sugar whenever you have to prepare a dish which uses fresh lemon juice and use lemon sugar in recipes that call for rind without the juice – bread and butter pudding, for example. Another use for lemon sugar is in sponges. It gives them a sharper and, to my mind, a pleasanter taste.

THE LARDER

We have become so accustomed to using refrigerators for every-day items and freezers for long-term storage that many of us have forgotten how useful an old-fashioned larder can be, especially for a family which eats a lot of puddings.

If you are moving house or have the chance to make alterations to your kitchen, do take the opportunity to find a house with a ready-made larder or have one built in. There is no better place to store such things as dry goods, a sack of potatoes, home-made jams and jellies and fresh butter at just the right temperature for baking.

And if you do not have a larder, what exactly do you do with a freshly baked apple pie or quiche that is too hot to put straight into the refrigerator? The larder is the perfect spot for such things, with the door firmly shut against children and dogs!

Flans, tarts and pies

All the recipes given here use pastry, thus making them extraordinarily versatile. They can be eaten hot or cold, as puddings accompanied by cream, custard or a special sauce, or as a teatime treat in place of the conventional cake. The difference between them lies in their shape and whether the pastry is used above or below the filling. Thus a flan is an open pastry case with vertical sides, either fluted or plain. It can be made with a flan ring which is removed after baking or in a flan dish where it remains for serving. A tart is usually baked in a plate, the pastry lining forming a flat rim to the filling which is placed in the hollow. A pie has a lid of pastry, placed over a deep oval or round dish with a flat rim to carry the pastry and, perhaps, an upturned egg-cup or ceramic pastry support, or even a handleless cup for a large pie, in the centre to hold up the pastry covering. Some pies are described as double crust, which means that pastry is used to line the dish and to cover the filling.

Open tarts and flans may be baked first and the filling added later. In this case, the pastry must be 'baked blind'; greaseproof paper is placed over the pastry lining and the dish filled with dried beans or rice to ensure that the pastry case keeps its shape. After cooking, the beans or rice are removed and when cool may be stored in a tin or jar to be used again. 'Baking blind' gives a crisper taste to the pastry base.

Most pies and flans freeze well. I always cook them first and freeze when cool. To use, allow the pie to thaw almost completely before reheating and serving. Unfilled flan cases may be frozen both cooked and uncooked. I prefer to cook them first as it saves time and trouble to reheat and use.

Uncooked home-made pastry is an excellent stand-by for the freezer. Pack in separate quantities of ½ lb and 1 lb (225 g and 450 g), labelling clearly, and thaw in the refrigerator or kitchen until it is pliable enough to roll and use. Bought pastry, such as puff pastry, is good and keeps well in the freezer.

APPLE PIE

Classic apple pie is always supposed to be a great favourite with men. I must say that, well made, there is really nothing to beat it. To prevent the pastry shrinking, chill the whole pie for 30 minutes before baking. I know that it is not correct but I always decorate my sweet pies with lots of pastry leaves; they look more inviting.

   1½ lb (675 g) cooking apples
   2 – 3 oz (50 g – 75 g) caster sugar
   4 cloves

Pastry:
   6 oz (175 g) plain flour
   1½ oz (40 g) margarine
   1½ oz (40 g) lard
   About 6 teaspoons cold water to mix

   Milk to glaze
   Granulated sugar

Put a pie funnel in the centre of a 1½-pint (900-ml) pie dish. Peel and core the apples and cut in thick slices; arrange half in the bottom of the pie dish, sprinkle with sugar and arrange the cloves evenly amongst the apple, cover with the remaining apple slices and add about 3 tablespoons cold water.

Sift the flour into a bowl and add the fats, cut into small pieces; rub in with fingertips until the mixture resembles fine breadcrumbs, then add sufficient cold water to mix to a firm dough. Roll out the pastry on a floured table and cover the top of the pie dish; use any trimmings to decorate if liked. Chill in the refrigerator for 30 minutes.

Heat the oven to 400°F, 200°C, gas no. 6. Brush the pie with a little milk and sprinkle the top with granulated sugar;

make a small slit in the centre for the steam to escape. Bake in the oven for 40 to 45 minutes until the apple is tender and the pastry crisp and pale golden brown.

Serves 4 – 6

MIDSUMMER FRUIT PIE

These are the sort of fruits that you have in a Summer Pudding. Serve hot with vanilla ice cream.

$\frac{1}{2}$ lb (225 g) rhubarb
$\frac{1}{4}$ lb (100 g) black currants
$\frac{1}{2}$ lb (225 g) raspberries
3 oz (75 g) caster sugar
2 tablespoons cold water

Pastry:
6 oz (175 g) plain flour
$1\frac{1}{2}$ oz (40 g) margarine
$1\frac{1}{2}$ oz (40 g) lard
About 6 teaspoons cold water

Milk to glaze
Granulated sugar

Put a pie funnel in the centre of a $1\frac{1}{2}$-pint (900-ml) pie dish. Cut the rhubarb into 1-inch (2.5-cm) lengths and mix all the fruits together; put half in the bottom of the pie dish and sprinkle with the sugar. Cover with the remaining fruit and add 2 tablespoons water.

Make the pastry up as usual (see Apple Pie, p. 9) and then roll out on a floured table and cover the top of the pie dish; use any trimmings to decorate if liked. Chill in the refrigerator for 30 minutes.

Heat the oven to 400°F, 200°C, gas no. 6. Brush the pie with a little milk and sprinkle the top with granulated sugar; make a small slit in the centre for the steam to escape. Bake in the oven for 40 to 45 minutes until the fruit is tender and the pastry crisp and a pale golden brown.

Serves 4 – 6

MINCEMEAT TART

Serve this all the year round, not just at Christmas. If I use bought mincemeat I often use a bit less and add some stewed apple to the mincemeat, which makes it less spicy and, I think, nicer. Brandy butter and whipped cream are an added luxury. I find the best hard margarine is Echo.

8 oz (225 g) strong plain flour
½ teaspoon salt
6 oz (175 g) hard margarine; chilled
About 9 tablespoons cold water or a scant ¼ pint
  (150 ml)
1-lb jar (411-g) mincemeat

Milk to glaze
Caster sugar

Sift the flour and salt into a mixing bowl. Coarsely grate the margarine into the bowl. Stir in just sufficient water to make a firm dough. Roll out on a lightly floured surface to make a strip about ½ inch thick and 6 inches (15 cm) wide. Fold pastry in three and give it a quarter turn to the left. Roll out again into a strip and fold in three. Wrap the pastry in foil and chill in the refrigerator for 30 minutes.

Heat the oven to 425°F, 220°C, gas no. 7.

Divide the pastry into two portions, one slightly larger than the other. Roll out smaller portion to ¼-inch thick circle and use it to line an 8-inch (20-cm) pie plate made of enamel or tin. Spoon the mincemeat into the dish.

Roll out the remaining pastry to a circle about ¼ inch thick. Brush the edges of the pastry already in the tin with milk and cover the mincemeat filling with the second pastry circle. Press edges together to seal and crimp to make a decorative finish, chill in the refrigerator for 10 minutes. Brush the top of the pie with a little milk and bake for 35 minutes, or until the pastry is golden brown and well risen. Sprinkle with sugar and serve warm.

Serves 6 – 8

BAKEWELL TART

This is not exactly the original recipe from Bakewell but I think it is easier to make and utterly delicious.

Pastry:
    6 oz (175 g) plain flour
    1½ oz (40 g) margarine
    1½ oz (40 g) lard
    About 6 teaspoons cold water.

Filling:
    1 heaped tablespoon raspberry or strawberry jam
    4 oz (100 g) butter
    4 oz (100 g) caster sugar
    1 egg, beaten
    4 oz (100 g) ground rice
    ½ teaspoon almond essence

Heat the oven to 400°F, 200°C, gas no. 6.

Make the pastry in the usual way (see recipe for Apple Pie p. 9). Roll out thinly on a floured table, line an 8-inch (20-cm) flan ring, which should be placed on a baking sheet, and prick the base with a fork; leave to rest in the refrigerator for 10 minutes.

Meanwhile prepare the filling: heat the butter in a saucepan until it has just melted but is not brown. Stir in the sugar and cook for one minute, then stir in the egg, ground rice and almond essence. Spread the jam over the base of the flan and pour filling on top. Roll out the pastry trimming and cut them into ¾-inch wide strips and arrange them in a lattice on top of the tart, making them stick with a little milk.

Bake in the oven for about 30 minutes until risen and golden brown, the filling should then spring back when lightly pressed with the finger. Take the tart out of the oven and remove the flan ring; leave to cool on a wire rack.

Serves 4 – 6

VICTORIAN TREACLE TART

This is a deep treacle tart that is not too sweet as it has added lemon. I find it best to warm the syrup and bread-crumbs, then you know exactly how much breadcrumbs the syrup will absorb – it does vary with the dryness of the bread before crumbing.

6 oz (175 g) plain flour
1½ oz (40 g) margarine
1½ oz (40 g) lard
About 6 teaspoons cold water to mix.
About 9 lightly rounded tablespoons golden syrup
About 9 rounded tablespoons fresh white breadcrumbs
Grated rind and juice of ½ a lemon

Put the flour in a bowl, add the fats, cut up in small pieces, and rub in with the finger tips until the mixture resembles fine breadcrumbs. Add sufficient cold water to mix to a firm dough. Roll out the pastry and line a 9-inch (22.5-cm) deep flan tin or sandwich tin. Leave in the refrigerator whilst preparing the filling.

Heat the oven to 400°F, 200°C, gas no. 6.

Warm the syrup in a saucepan until runny and stir in the breadcrumbs. Leave to stand for 10 minutes or until the crumbs have absorbed the syrup, then stir in the lemon rind and juice. As it is difficult to be accurate when measuring golden syrup add a little more syrup if the mixture looks too thick or more breadcrumbs if the mixture appears to be a little runny.

Pour the filling into the pastry case and bake in the oven for 10 minutes, then reduce the heat to 375°F, 190°C, gas no. 5 and bake for a further 15 minutes or until the tart is cooked. Leave to cool in the tin for a little while and then serve warm with lots of thick cream or ice cream.

Serves about 8 portions

FRENCH APPLE FLAN

This is a very professional looking flan, especially attractive for a buffet table.

    4 oz (100 g) plain flour
    1½ oz (40 g) butter
    1 oz (25 g) lard
    1 egg yolk
    ½ oz (12½ g) caster sugar
    About 1 teaspoon cold water

Filling:
    1 lb (450 g) cooking apples
    2 tablespoons cold water
    About 2 tablespoons granulated sugar
    Apricot jam
    1 red skinned eating apple, for topping

First make the pastry: put the flour in a bowl, add the fats, cut in small pieces, and rub in with the finger tips until the mixture resembles fine breadcrumbs. Mix the egg yolk with the sugar and water and stir into the dry ingredients and bind them together. Roll out the pastry on a floured table and line a 7-inch (17.5-cm) flan ring, on a baking sheet. Chill for 30 minutes.

Heat the oven to 425°F, 220°C, gas no. 7. Line the flan with greaseproof paper and weigh down with baking beans and bake blind for 15 minutes.

Meanwhile prepare the filling; wash the apples; quarter, core and slice into a saucepan with the water; cover and cook gently until the apples are soft and fluffy, about 15 minutes, stirring occasionally to prevent catching. Sieve the apples into a bowl and stir in the sugar to sweeten to taste.

Remove the beans and greaseproof paper from the flan and spoon in the apple filling.

Warm a little apricot jam in a saucepan so that it will form a glaze, if necessary add a little water and sieve to make it smooth.

Cut the eating apple into quarters, core and thinly slice. Arrange attractively on top of the purée and brush with apricot glaze.

Return the flan to the oven, reduce the temperature to 350°F, 180°C, gas no. 4 and bake for a further 20 to 25 minutes, until the pastry is pale brown and the slices of apple are cooked. Serve warm or cold with cream.

Serves 4 – 6

LEMON MERINGUE PIE

If your family adores lemon meringue pie and you are short of time, instead of doing it in a pastry flan case use a bought sponge flan as a base. Put three yolks in the filling and use the whites for the meringue.

6 oz (175 g) plain flour
2 oz (50 g) butter
2 oz (50 g) lard
1 egg yolk
½ oz (12½ g) caster sugar
2 teaspoons cold water

Lemon filling:
2 large lemons
1½ oz (40 g) cornflour
½ pint (300 ml) water

2 egg yolks
3 oz (75 g) caster sugar

Meringue topping:
3 egg whites
4½ oz (125 g) caster sugar

First make the pastry: put the flour in a bowl, add the fats, cut into small pieces, and rub in with the finger tips until the mixture resembles fine breadcrumbs. Mix the egg yolk, sugar and water together and stir into the dry ingredients and bind them together. Roll out the pastry on a floured board and line a 9-inch (22.5-cm) flan tin. Chill for 30 minutes.

Heat the oven to 425°F, 220°C, gas no. 7 with a thick baking sheet in it. Line the flan with greaseproof paper and weigh down with baking beans and bake blind for 15 minutes.

Meanwhile prepare the filling: finely grate the rind and squeeze the juice from the lemons and put in a bowl with the cornflour; add 2 tablespoons of the water and blend to form a smooth paste. Boil the remaining water and pour it onto the cornflour mixture, return it to the pan, bring to the boil and simmer for 3 minutes until thick, stirring continuously. Remove from the heat and add the egg yolks blended with sugar, return to the heat for a moment to thicken the sauce and then cool slightly.

Remove the beans and greaseproof paper from the flan and spoon in the filling.

Whisk the egg whites with an electric or rotary whisk until they form stiff peaks, add the sugar a teaspoonful at a time, whisking well after each addition. Spoon the meringue over the lemon filling, being careful to spread it right up to the edge of the pastry, leaving no air spaces. Return the pie to the oven and reduce the heat to 325°F, 160°C, gas no. 3 for about 30 minutes or until a pale golden brown. Serve the pie either warm or cold.

Serves 6

LEMON CREAM TART

This is my life-saver pud. Thomas my eldest son always calls it 'his' as he often makes it, mainly because he likes it and once made it on television. It takes 10 minutes to make and if it is for children I decorate the top with lemon sugared slices; for grown-ups I usually arrange halved grapes around the edge. Well worth trying, you really can't taste the condensed milk!

    4 oz (100 g) digestive biscuits
    2 oz (50 g) butter
    1 oz (25 g) demerara sugar
    8 oz (225 g) cream cheese
    Large can condensed milk
    Grated rind and juice of 2 large lemons
    A few grapes or sugared lemon slices to decorate

Put the biscuits in a polythene bag and crush with a rolling pin. Melt the butter in a small pan, add the sugar and stir in the biscuit crumbs and mix well. Turn into an 8-inch (20-cm) flan dish and press into shape around the base and sides with the back of a spoon.

Put the cream cheese in a bowl and cream until light and soft, then beat in the condensed milk with the lemon rind and juice. Pour into the flan case and leave to set.

Decorate with halved grapes or lemon slices.

Serves 6

GOOSEBERRY SHORTCAKE

This makes a nice change from the usual fruit pie or crumble.

    6 oz (175 g) butter
    3 oz (75 g) caster sugar
    6 oz (175 g) self-raising flour
    3 oz (75 g) cornflour
    8 oz (225 g) gooseberries
    1 oz (25 g) walnuts, chopped
    1 oz (25 g) demerara sugar

Heat the oven to 375°F, 190°C, gas no. 5 and grease a 7-inch (17.5-cm) square shallow tin.

Cream the butter and sugar together until light and fluffy. Sift the flour and cornflour together and add to the butter, work in and then knead together. Turn the mixture onto a table and knead lightly for 3 minutes or until the mixture is smooth.

Reserve one-third of the mixture and spread the rest evenly over the base of the tin–use the flat of your hand to do this.

Cover with the gooseberries. Add the walnuts and demerara sugar to the reserved mixture and knead lightly until mixed, roughly pat out to the size of the tin and spread over the gooseberries.

Bake in the oven for 45 minutes or until the gooseberries are cooked and the topping lightly browned. It is best served warm with cream.

Serves 6

OPEN APRICOT TART

The French always make the most lavish looking tarts; this
is one of the classics and it is worthwhile making a big one
as it takes time to do. No-one minds if there is some left for
the next day.

Pastry:
    6 oz (175 g) plain flour
    2 oz (50 g) butter
    2 oz (50 g) lard
    Pinch salt
    1 egg yolk
    ½ oz (12½ g) caster sugar
    2 teaspoons water

Filling:
    2 eggs
    1½ oz (40 g) caster sugar
    1 oz (25 g) flour
    ¼ pint (150 ml) milk, plus 4 tablespoons
    A few drops of vanilla essence
    14½-oz (411-g) can apricots
    1½ level teaspoons arrowroot
    ¼ pint (150 ml) apricot juice, from the can
    1 tablespoon brandy (optional)
    A few toasted flaked almonds

Heat the oven to 400°F, 200°C, gas no. 6. Make the pastry as
for Lemon Meringue Pie (see p. 16) and line a 9-inch (22.5-
cm) fluted flan tin and bake blind for 15 minutes, then
remove the beans and greaseproof paper and cook for a
further 5 to 10 minutes to dry out the centre. Leave to cool.

Meanwhile make the filling: mix the eggs, sugar and flour
together, boil the milk and add to the egg mixture, stirring.
Return to the pan and simmer for 2 to 3 minutes until thick,

remove from the heat and stir frequently whilst cooling so that a skin does not form. Stir in the vanilla essence and spread over the base of the flan.

Drain the apricots and arrange on top of the custard. Put the arrowroot in a small saucepan and stir in ¼ pint (150 ml) apricot juice and bring to the boil, stirring until thickened and clear. Add the brandy if used. Spoon the glaze over the apricots and leave to set. Scatter with almonds.

Serves 8

MINCEMEAT AND ALMOND PIE

This is such a good pudding – rather special in fact. It is best served warm with brandy butter or whipped cream.

 ¾ lb (350 g) cooking apples
 7 oz (200 g) light soft brown sugar
 1 tablespoon water
 ½ lb (225 g) mincemeat
 4 oz (100 g) soft margarine
 4 oz (100 g) ground almonds
 2 eggs, beaten
 ½ oz (12½ g) flaked almonds

Heat the oven to 350°F, 180°C, gas no. 4.

Peel, core and slice the apples and put in a saucepan with 3 oz (75 g) soft brown sugar and the water and stew gently until tender. Stir in the mincemeat and turn into a pie dish.

Put the remaining sugar, margarine, ground almonds and eggs in a bowl and beat well. Spread over the apple mixture and then sprinkle with flaked almonds and bake in the oven for 1 hour, on which time the mixture will be firm to the touch and golden brown.

Serve hot or warm.

Serves 5 – 6

ENGLISH CUSTARD TART

To get the base of the pastry really cooked through and brown stand the tart when filled on a thick baking sheet that has been thoroughly heated up in the oven first. This means that as soon as the tart tin touches the hot baking sheet it begins to cook. If you like a richer pastry use the rich shortcrust in French Apple Flan, page 15.

Shortcrust pastry:
   4 oz (100 g) plain flour
   1 oz (25 g) margarine
   1 oz (25 g) lard
   About 4 teaspoons cold water

Custard:
   2 eggs
   1 oz (25 g) caster sugar
   ½ pint (300 ml) milk
   A little grated nutmeg

Heat the oven, with a baking sheet in it, to 400°F, 200°C, gas no. 6. Prepare the pastry as usual (see Apple Pie, p. 9) and roll out and line an enamel, tin or foil 7-inch (17.5-cm) flan tin; chill.

For the custard, beat the eggs and sugar together until blended and then stir in the milk. Pour into the pastry case and sprinkle with a little nutmeg. Place on the hot baking sheet in the oven and cook for 15 minutes, then reduce the heat to 350°F, 180°C, gas no. 4 and bake for a further 25 minutes or until the filling is set and a pale golden brown.

Serve warm on the day that it is made.

Serves 4 – 6

Traditional winter puddings

If you are on a diet, skip to the next chapter! If you are not, this is a chance to indulge in those marvellously filling schoolboy puddings which were the downfall of Billy Bunter! Remember that they take time to cook – you can't decide to make one of them just as you're laying the table for dinner!

They will all freeze well, but I rarely do so because they take up room in the freezer and need almost as much time to reheat as they do to cook. The only exception is Christmas pudding if I make too many and want to keep the surplus until next year.

TREACLE SUET PUDDING –
made, of course, with golden syrup

This is the perfect pudding for a really cold day. Out of all the suet puds our favourite is treacle. If apples are plentiful I often put a layer of sliced ones, with a little brown sugar, between two layers of suet pudding so that when you turn the pudding out you get a treacle top and a centre layer of apple, which makes it even more enjoyable. When turning the pudding out use a deepish dish to catch the syrup.

3 rounded tablespoons golden syrup, generous
   measure!
4 oz (100 g) self-raising flour
4 oz (100 g) fresh white breadcrumbs
4 oz (100 g) shredded suet
2 oz (50 g) caster sugar
About 4 fluid oz (120 ml) milk

Grease a 1½-pint (900-ml) pudding basin and put the syrup in the bottom. Put the flour, breadcrumbs, suet and sugar in a bowl and mix lightly, then stir in sufficient milk to mix to a medium dropping consistency. Put the mixture into the bowl and cover with a piece of greased greaseproof paper with a pleat in the centre and a lid of foil. Steam or boil for about 2–3 hours. If boiling, place the bowl on an upturned saucer in a saucepan with boiling water which comes half-way up the sides of the basin. In either case keep an eye on the water level and top up with boiling water during cooking if necessary.

Remove the foil and greaseproof paper and turn out onto a warm dish and serve with a little extra warmed syrup or custard.

Serves 4 – 6

JANE GRIGSON'S SUSSEX POND PUDDING

Jane is a great authority on historical food; this recipe is, as Jane says, the best of all English boiled puddings. In the middle the butter and sugar melt to a rich sauce, which is sharpened with the juice from the lemon. The genius of the pudding is the lemon. Its citrus bitter flavour is a subtlety which raises the pudding to the highest class. When you serve it, make sure that everyone has a piece of lemon, which will be much softened by the cooking but still vigorous. The name of the pudding refers to the sauce which runs out of it, when it is turned onto a serving dish, and provides it with a moat of buttery brown liquid. It seems a lot of butter and sugar but it makes all the difference.

    8 oz (225 g) self-raising flour
    4 oz (100 g) shredded suet
    Approximately ¼ pint (150 ml) milk and water mixed
    6 oz (175 g) butter
    6 oz (175 g) demerara sugar
    1 large lemon

Mix the flour and suet together in a bowl and add sufficient milk and water to mix to a soft dough. Turn out onto a lightly floured table and knead gently. Cut off a quarter of the dough and put on one side. Roll out the remaining dough and use to line a greased 1½-pint (900-ml) pudding basin. Cut the butter in small pieces and mix with the sugar. Prick the lemon all over and stand upright in the centre of the pudding basin. Put the butter and sugar mixture around it. Roll out the remaining dough to a circle the size of the top of the basin, damp the edges and cover the pudding. Seal firmly.

Cover with a piece of greased greaseproof paper with a pleat in the centre and a lid of foil and steam for 3–4 hours (see Treacle Suet Pudding, p. 27). Run a knife around the edge of the pudding and turn out onto a warm serving dish. Make sure that each portion is garnished with a slice of lemon from inside the pudding.

Serves 4

BLACKBERRY AND APPLE PUDDING

Make as above but fill the centre with a mixture of 1 lb (450 g) cooking apples, peeled, cored and thinly sliced and 6 – 8 oz (175 g – 225 g) blackberries and 3 oz (75 g) sugar. Serve hot with custard.

Serves 4

RADLEY PUDDING

A real schoolboy winter pudding. Make sure that there is plenty of golden syrup or custard to pour over, though some may prefer brown sugar and cream.

- $\frac{1}{4}$ – $\frac{1}{2}$ level teaspoon cinnamon
- 4 oz (100 g) demerara sugar
- 8 oz (225 g) peeled chunks of raw cooking apples
- 8 oz (225 g) self-raising flour
- 4 oz (100 g) prepared shredded suet
- 10 – 12 tablespoons cold water

Stir the cinnamon into the demerara sugar and roll the apple pieces in the sugar, making sure that they are well coated.

Mix the flour with the suet and stir in the apple and sugar mixture. Add just sufficient water to mix to make a light and soft, but not sticky, dough.

Turn into a well greased 2-pint (a good litre) basin. Cover the top with a piece of greased greaseproof paper with a pleat in the centre and a lid of double foil.

Place in a saucepan, add sufficient boiling water to come half-way up the sides of the basin and cover the saucepan and boil gently for about 3 hours, topping up with more boiling water if necessary (see Treacle Suet Pudding, p. 27).

Turn out and serve hot with golden syrup or custard.

Serves 8

APPLE AND APRICOT STEAMED PUDDING

This is a good variation on the apple theme; the bread-crumbs give an extra light texture.

    6 oz (175 g) self-raising flour
    2 oz (50 g) fresh white breadcrumbs
    4 oz (100 g) shredded suet
    10 tablespoons milk
    4 oz (100 g) dried apricots soaked over night and then
      drained
    1 lb (450 g) cooking apples, peeled and sliced
    4 oz (100 g) soft brown sugar

Butter a 2-pint (1-l) pudding basin. Put the flour, bread-crumbs and suet in a bowl. Add sufficient milk to make a soft dough and divide into three portions, in graded sizes. Roll out the smallest portion to line the base of the basin. Add half of the apricots, apples and sugar, then roll out the second portion of pastry to fit over the fruit. Put the remaining fruit on top and cover with the remaining pastry rolled to fit the basin.

Cover with a greased and pleated lid of greaseproof paper and a lid of foil. Steam or boil for about 3 hours (see Treacle Suet Pudding, p. 27), then turn out onto a warm serving plate and serve with a custard sauce.

Serves 6

CHRISTMAS PLUM PUDDING

When the pudding is cooked, cool, cover with fresh foil then store in a cool larder until Christmas day, then simmer for a further 3 hours. Serve with plenty of brandy butter or cream.

$\frac{1}{2}$ level teaspoon mixed spice
8 oz (225 g) mixed dried fruit
4 oz (100 g) stoned raisins
3 oz (75 g) shredded suet
4 oz (100 g) dark soft brown sugar
5 oz (150 g) fresh brown breadcrumbs
3 oz (75 g) carrot
1 small cooking apple
1 rounded tablespoon marmalade
2 eggs, beaten

Well grease a 2-pint (a good litre) basin. Put the spice, fruit, suet, sugar and breadcrumbs into a large bowl. Peel the carrot and apple and coarsely grate into the bowl. Add the marmalade and beaten eggs and mix thoroughly.

Turn into the prepared basin and cover with a double layer of greased foil, carefully putting a pleat in the middle of the foil to allow for expansion of the pudding during cooking. Stand in a pan of water to come half way up the basin. Cover pan and simmer for 7 hours, or cook in a steamer. Keep a check on the water level so that it does not boil dry and top up with extra boiling water if necessary.

Take out the pudding and leave to cool. Cover with a fresh piece of foil and store in a cool place until Christmas day. Then simmer for a further 3 hours before serving.

For a final dramatic effect, heat up a little brandy, pour over the pudding and set a light.

Serves 8

BAKED JAM ROLY POLY

I have to confess that I love it either with jam or mincemeat. Thank goodness it is something that one makes rarely as it is so good and so fattening!

8 oz (225 g) self-raising flour
Pinch of salt
4 oz (100 g) shredded suet
About 7 – 8 tablespoons cold water to mix
5 heaped tablespoons strawberry or raspberry jam

Heat the oven to 425°F, 220°C, gas no. 7 and lightly flour a baking tray.

Mix together the flour, salt and suet in a bowl and add sufficient cold water to make a soft but not sticky dough and then knead lightly.

Roll out on a floured surface to an 8-inch (20-cm) square and spread the jam to within 1 inch (2.5 cm) of the edge, roll up loosely and press the edges firmly together with a rolling pin.

Lift onto the baking tray and cook for about 30 minutes or until golden brown. Serve hot with custard.

Serves 6

SPOTTED DICK

A very warming winter pudding, especially good when served with warmed golden syrup.

4 oz (100 g) self-raising flour
4 oz (100 g) fresh white breadcrumbs
4 oz (100 g) shredded suet
2 oz (50 g) caster sugar
3 oz (75 g) currants
Finely grated rind of 1 lemon
About ¼ pint (150 ml) milk

Put the flour, breadcrumbs, suet, sugar, currants and lemon rind in a bowl and mix well. Then add sufficient milk to make a medium dropping consistency.

Well grease a 1½-pint (900-ml) pudding basin and put in the mixture. Cover with a piece of greased greaseproof paper with a pleat in the centre, to allow for rising, and a cover of foil.

Steam or boil for about 2–3 hours. If boiling place on an upturned saucer in a saucepan with boiling water coming half-way up the sides of the basin. In either case keep an eye on the water level and top up with boiling water during cooking if necessary.

Remove the lids and turn out onto a warmed plate and serve with warmed golden syrup or custard sauce.

Serves 4 – 6

CHOCOLATE PUDDING

A very filling sponge pudding for the really hungry who have memories of chocolate pudding at school.

4 oz (100 g) soft margarine
4 oz (100 g) caster sugar
2 eggs

4 oz (100 g) self-raising flour
½ oz (12½ g) cocoa
1 level teaspoon baking powder
3 tablespoons milk

Sauce:
1 level tablespoon cocoa
2 level tablespoons cornflour
2 oz (50 g) caster sugar
½ pint (300 ml) milk

Grease a 1¼-pint (750-ml) oven-proof dish. Put the margarine, sugar and eggs into a bowl and sift in the flour, cocoa and baking powder; add the milk and beat well for about 2 minutes until thoroughly blended. Turn into the dish and bake in the oven at 350°F, 180°C, gas no. 4 for about 45 minutes until just risen and firm to the touch.

Meanwhile prepare the sauce: put the cocoa, cornflour and sugar in a small saucepan and gradually stir in the milk to make a smooth blend. Place over a moderate heat and bring to the boil, stirring continually until the mixture thickens. Then simmer for a minute and serve hot over slices of sponge pudding.

Serves 4

EVE'S PUDDING

I rarely make this pudding without doubling the Eve sponge part and using half for a sponge sandwich for tea or I add some fruit for buns and bake them at the same time as the pudding. The half quantity will make two 7-inch

(17.5-cm) sponge sandwiches or about 18 buns in fairly
deep bun tins.

  1 lb (450 g) cooking apples, peeled, cored and sliced
  3 oz (75 g) demerara sugar
  Grated rind and juice of 1 lemon
  4 oz (100 g) soft margarine
  4 oz (100 g) caster sugar
  2 eggs
  4 oz (100 g) self-raising flour
  1 level teaspoon baking powder

Heat the oven to 350°F, 180°C, gas no. 4. Grease a 2-pint (a
good litre) oven-proof dish, and put in the apples. Sprinkle
with demerara sugar and the lemon rind and juice.

Put the margarine, sugar, eggs, flour and baking powder in
a bowl and beat well for a minute until well blended.
Spread over the apples and bake in the centre of the oven
for about 1 hour. Test by pressing with a finger; if done the
sponge will spring back when lightly touched.

Serve hot with custard.

Serves 6

STEAMED SPONGE PUDDING

A great family favourite for a cold winter's day. I use plum
jam as I think it is best, but any will do.

  4 tablespoons jam, generous measure!
  1 tablespoon water
  4 oz (100 g) soft margarine
  4 oz (100 g) caster sugar
  2 eggs

   4 oz (100 g) self-raising flour
   1 level teaspoon baking powder

Grease a 1½-pint (900-ml) pudding basin. Blend the jam with the water and put it at the bottom of the basin. Place all the remaining ingredients together in a bowl and beat well for about 2 minutes or until well blended.

Spoon into the pudding basin and smooth the top. Cover the top with a piece of greased greaseproof paper with a pleat in the centre and a lid of double foil.

Put in a steamer over a pan of hot water and steam gently for about 2 hours. Turn out and serve at once.

Serves 4

APRICOT AND LEMON PUDDING

Make as above but use apricot jam and blend with 1 tablespoon lemon juice instead of water and add the grated rind of a lemon to the sponge mixture.

Serves 4

BLACKCURRANT UPSIDE DOWN PUDDING

A quick and easy pudding to make, that looks very good when turned out.

   6 oz (175 g) blackcurrants
   2 level tablespoons granulated sugar

Sponge:
  2 oz (50 g) soft margarine
  2 oz (50 g) caster sugar
  1 large egg, beaten
  3 oz (75 g) self-raising flour
  Milk

Grease a 1¼-pint (750-ml) oven-proof dish, that is about 2 –
3 inches (5–7.5 cm) deep. Heat the oven to 350°F, 180°C,
gas no. 4.

Toss the black currants and granulated sugar together and
put in the bottom of the dish.

Cream the margarine and sugar until light and fluffy and
then beat in the egg a little at a time, fold in the flour and
add sufficient milk, about 1 tablespoonful, to make a soft
dropping consistency. Spread over the black currants and
bake in the oven for about 45 minutes or until the sponge is
well risen and golden brown. Turn out onto a dish and
serve hot with custard.

Serves 4

APPLE CHARLOTTE

A good pudding to use up a glut of apples; very popular in
the school holidays. For the grown-ups add cinnamon to
the apple and for a change use thin slices of brown bread
instead of white. Choose a fairly shallow dish to cook it in
so that there is lots of brown crispy topping.

  6 – 7 thin slices white bread from a large loaf
  3 oz (75 g) butter
  1½ lb (675 g) cooking apples

3 oz (75 g) light soft brown or demerara sugar
2 tablespoons water

Heat the oven to 400°F, 200°C, gas no. 6 and butter a shallow 2-pint (a good litre) oven-proof dish. Spread the bread thinly with butter on one side and with a 2-inch (5-cm) cutter stamp out four rounds from each slice of bread. Arrange the bread over the sides and base of the dish, reserving a few circles for the top.

Peel, core and slice the apples and place in a saucepan with the sugar and water, cover and cook gently until soft and thick, then beat with a wooden spoon until smooth. Spoon into the dish and cover the top with the remaining circles of bread. Sprinkle the top with a little extra brown sugar and bake in the oven for 25 to 30 minutes until the bread is crisp and golden brown. Serve piping hot with thin cream or ice cream.

Serves 4

APPLE WITH BROWN SUGAR CRUMBLE

Most fruits from the garden are good for a crumble, especially plums, gooseberries and rhubarb.

6 oz (175 g) plain flour
1½ oz (40 g) margarine
1½ oz (40 g) lard
2 oz (50 g) brown sugar
1½ lb (675 g) cooking apples
4 oz (100 g) caster sugar
2 tablespoons water

Heat the oven to 400°F, 200°C, gas no. 6.

Sift the flour into a bowl and add the fat cut in small pieces. Rub in with the fingertips until the mixture resembles fine breadcrumbs. Stir in the brown sugar.

Peel, core and slice the apples and put in layers into a 1¾-pint (1-l) pie dish with the caster sugar and water. Pile the crumble on top so that it completely covers the apples and bake in the oven for about 45 minutes until the fruit is cooked and the crumble golden brown. If using cooked apple bake for 30 minutes.

Serve hot with custard or cream and extra demerara sugar if liked.

Serves 4

QUEEN OF PUDDINGS

An old-fashioned pud that is well worth making again. It is a set custard made with yolks and added breadcrumbs; this is then spread with warmed strawberry jam. If your strawberry jam is a bit runny there is no need to warm it! Finally it is topped with whisked egg whites. When my mother used to make it I remember she strained off the lemon rind, but I prefer it in the custard as long as it is finely grated.

1 pint (600 ml) milk
1 oz (25 g) butter
2 oz (50 g) caster sugar
Finely grated rind of 1 lemon
4 egg yolks
3 oz (75 g) fresh white breadcrumbs
3 tablespoons strawberry jam

Topping:
  4 egg whites
  6 oz (175 g) caster sugar

Heat the oven to 350°F, 180°C, gas no. 4 and grease a 2-pint (a good litre) pie dish.

Warm the milk in a small saucepan, then add the butter, sugar and lemon rind, stir lightly so that the sugar dissolves and the butter melts. Whisk the egg yolks in a small bowl and gradually whisk on the warmed milk. Put the bread-crumbs in the pie dish and pour over the warm milk. Leave to stand for 15 minutes then bake in the oven for about 25 to 30 minutes or until just set. Remove from the oven and spread the warmed jam over the custard.

Whisk the egg whites until stiff with an electric or hand rotary whisk and then whisk in the sugar a teaspoonful at a time. Pile onto the pudding and spread right to the edge of the dish, so that it completely covers the custard, and roughly peak. Return to the oven and bake for a further 10 to 15 minutes until the meringue is just tinged a pale golden brown all over. Serve at once with cream.

Serves 6

BREAD AND BUTTER PUDDING

Definitely one of my favourite family puddings. We often have it after a cold meat, or maybe a fairly lean, first course when everyone is still famished.

About 4 oz (100 g) butter
12 thin slices white bread with the crusts removed
6 oz (175 g) mixed dried fruit
Grated rind of 2 lemons
4 oz (100 g) demerara sugar
1 pint (600 ml) milk
2 eggs

Butter very thoroughly a shallow 3-pint (1.7-l) oven-proof dish. Melt the butter in a saucepan and dip the bread into it, coating one side with butter; this is a much quicker way than spreading each slice with butter. Cut each slice in three and arrange half the bread, butter side down, in the dish.

Cover with half of the fruit, lemon rind and sugar and top with the remaining bread, butter side uppermost. Sprinkle with the rest of the fruit, lemon rind and sugar.

Blend the milk and eggs together and strain over the pudding. Leave it to stand for at least an hour – but it is better if left for about 2 to 3 hours.

Heat the oven to 350°F, 180°C, gas no. 4 and bake for 40 minutes until puffy and a pale golden brown and set firm.

Serve at once.

Serves 6 – 8

MARY NORWAK'S BREAD PUDDING

Mary Norwak gave me this recipe; it is the best bread pudding that I have ever tasted. Use the crusts in the pudding too; if you have the odd stale bun or roll use it instead of bread slices.

8 slices white bread (toast thickness)
½ pint (300 ml) milk
12 oz (350 g) mixed dried fruit
2 oz (50 g) mixed chopped peel
1 apple, peeled and grated
3 oz (75 g) light soft brown sugar
3 oz (75 g) self-raising flour
2 rounded tablespoons marmalade
2 eggs
Juice of half a lemon
1 level teaspoon ground cinnamon
4 oz (100 g) butter or margarine

Soak the bread with the crusts on in the milk until really soft. Heat the oven to 300°F, 150°C, gas no. 3. Grease a meat roasting tin 11 inches × 7 inches (28 cm × 17.5 cm).

Add the fruit, peel, apple, sugar, flour, marmalade, eggs, lemon juice and cinnamon to the bread and beat thoroughly until well mixed.

Melt the butter in a small saucepan and stir half into the pudding mixture, then turn into the prepared tin and drizzle the remaining butter over the top. Bake in the oven for 1½ hours and then raise the heat to 350°F, 180°C, gas no. 4 and bake for a further 30 minutes until golden brown.

Serve hot with custard or, sprinkled with icing sugar, cold as a cake.

Serves 8

BAKED APPLE DUMPLINGS

I think true apple dumplings are apples wrapped in suet crust pastry, but we prefer apples wrapped in short crust pastry.

10 oz (275 g) plain flour
2½ oz (62½ g) margarine
2½ oz (62½ g) lard
About 3 tablespoons cold water
4 medium -sized cooking apples, peeled and cored
1½ oz (40 g) demerara sugar or dark soft brown sugar
1½ oz (40 g) sultanas or raisins
A good pinch cinnamon
Milk

Heat the oven to 400°F, 200°C, gas no. 6.

Make the pastry (see Apple Pie, p. 9) and divide into four equal pieces. Roll each piece into a 7-inch (17.5-cm) circle.

Put an apple into the centre of each pastry round. Mix the sugar, fruit and cinnamon together and use to fill the centre of each apple. Bring the edges of the pastry together over the apples and, trimming neatly if necessary, press to a smooth shape. Put them on a lightly greased baking sheet with the sealed edges underneath. Make a hole in the centre top of each dumpling.

Roll out any pastry trimming and use to make leaves with which to decorate the dumplings. Brush with milk and bake in the oven for 35 to 45 minutes until lightly browned.

Sprinkle with a little granulated sugar and serve warm with custard.

Serves 4

BRANDY BUTTER

Make this butter to go with mincepies and Christmas pudding; any left can be kept in the freezer for up to 3 months.

½ lb (225 g) unsalted butter
½ lb (225 g) icing sugar
6 tablespoons brandy

Cream the butter with a wooden spoon until it is soft. Gradually beat in the icing sugar and continue beating until the mixture is light and fluffy, then beat in the brandy.

Turn the butter into a serving dish and chill in the refrigerator to harden before serving. If made in advance it is good idea to leave the brandy butter at room temperature for 30 minutes before required.

BRANDY CREAM

If you want something a little lighter, try this cream for a change.

¼ pint (150 ml) double cream
1 tablespoon caster sugar
2 tablespoons brandy

Put all the ingredients together in a bowl and whisk them together until thick and the mixture forms soft peaks. Pile it into a bowl and serve slightly chilled.

REAL THICK POURING CREAM

Cream is now sadly expensive. At the weekends I make this cream in the blender, it tastes extremely good, no one has ever commented that it is not fresh cream. Of course it really is cream because it is reconstituted from fresh unsalted butter. The result is about half the price of cream from the shops. I use it in recipes that call for single cream and it only takes about 30 seconds in the blender.

½ lb (225 g) unsalted butter
½ pint (300 ml) milk
Scant level teaspoon powdered gelatine

Cut the butter into small pieces. Put the milk in a pan and sprinkle on the gelatine and leave for 3 minutes. Add the butter and heat until the butter has just melted. Pour into the blender and switch on to maximum for 30 seconds until blended. Pour into a jug and chill before serving cold after stirring. These quantities make just under 1 pint (568 ml) cream.

Pancakes, batters and fritters

These recipes are all made from the same basic mixture of flour, egg and milk, although the ratio of ingredients and additional flavourings depend on the purpose for which the mixture is intended. The variations are given in the individual recipes.

Uncooked batter will keep well in the refrigerator for a couple of days. To freeze cooked pancakes, separate each pancake with greaseproof paper, pack in foil and freeze. I find that it is best to cook pancakes when children are at school. If I try to cook extra when they are at home, with the intention of freezing the surplus, there never seem to be any left! Why do children's appetites expand in direct proportion to the number of pancakes on the plate?

PANCAKES

To me the best pancakes are those that come straight from
the pan to a waiting hot plate and are served with sugar and
a good wedge of lemon. They are a perfect pudding and are
made from basic ingredients which are nearly always to
hand. For the children I have given up making them wafer
thin because they can quite easily down six or seven at one
sitting. I make them slightly thicker and they seem to enjoy
them just as much and I am not endlessly making them at
the stove.

Pancakes can be made ahead for stuffing and for Crêpes
Suzette. As I make each one I put them out singly on
kitchen paper to cool and then stack them carefully. If you
are careful and handle them lightly there is no need to
separate them with a piece of greaseproof paper between
each one. Reheat covered with foil in a moderate oven for
about 20 minutes for a pile of eight or ten or reheat in butter
in a frying pan.

To freeze: pack in convenient numbers (four to eight are
just enough for one meal). Wrap each batch in foil. If you
are likely to want to use them without thawing them first
put a piece of greaseproof paper or foil between each pan-

cake, then with care you can prise them apart while they are still frozen.

CLASSIC PANCAKES

Caster sugar
4 oz (100 g) plain flour
¼ teaspoon salt
1 egg, beaten
½ pint (300 ml) milk and water mixed
1 tablespoon salad oil
Oil for frying
Lemon juice

Sprinkle caster sugar on a sheet of greaseproof paper and put on one side. Sift flour and salt into a mixing bowl and make a well in the centre. Add the egg and gradually stir in half the milk and water mixture. Using a whisk blend in the flour from the sides of the bowl. Beat well until the mixture is smooth. Stir in the remaining milk liquid and salad oil.

Heat a little oil in a 7- or 8-inch frying pan. When it is hot pour off any excess oil and spoon about 2 tablespoons of the batter into the pan. Tip and rotate the pan so that the batter spreads out and thinly covers the bottom of the pan. Cook the pancake for about 1 minute until pale brown underneath, then turn it over with a palette knife and cook for another minute.

Invert the pancake onto sugared paper, sprinkle with lemon juice and roll up. Place on a hot serving dish and keep warm whilst making more in the same way.

Makes 8 – 10 pancakes

ANN'S CINNAMON AND APPLE PANCAKES

These are simply delicious recipes given to me by a friend who is very creative and ingenious whether on a boat, or a tiny cooker in a holiday house or at home.

8 – 10 pancakes

Filling:
　4 large Bramley apples, peeled and cored and sliced
　$\frac{1}{4}$ teaspoon ground cinnamon
　6 oz (175 g) demerara sugar
　6 oz (175 g) butter

Put the pancakes on one side. Put the apples in a saucepan and gently cook with, cinnamon, sugar and 4 oz (100 g) of butter, stirring occasionally, for about 20 minutes or until the apples are tender and the mixture is a thick pulp. Spread the pancakes on a flat surface and spoon some of the apple filling on to each and roll them up.

Melt the remaining butter in a large frying pan, and fry the rolled-up pancakes on all sides until they are brown. Pile on a warm serving dish and sprinkle with a little extra sugar and cinnamon. Serve hot with lots of cream or ice cream.

8 – 10 pancakes

APRICOT AND ALMOND PANCAKES

Prepare as above but use about $1\frac{1}{4}$ lb (550 g) fresh apricots, halved and stoned and when frying the rolls add 1 oz (25 g) flaked almonds to the pan and toss these over the pancake rolls after putting them on a serving dish.

BRAMBLE AND APPLE PANCAKES

These are good when blackberries are in season, or try using a black currant and apple mixture.

8 – 10 pancakes

Filling:
 1 lb (450 g) cooking apples, peeled, cored and sliced
 ½ lb (225 g) blackberries
 4 oz (100 g) granulated sugar
 4 oz (100 g) butter
 1 level tablespoon cornflour
 1 tablespoon water

Spread the pancakes on a flat surface.

For the filling: put the apples, blackberries, sugar and 2 oz (50 g) butter in a pan and simmer gently for about 20 minutes or until the apple is tender. Blend the cornflour with the water and stir into the apple mixture. Cook for 2 minutes or until the mixture has thickened. Leave to cool.

Divide the mixture between the pancakes and roll up.

Melt the remaining butter in a larg frying pan and fry the rolled up pancakes on all sides until they are brown. Pile on a warm serving dish and sprinkle with a little extra granulated sugar and serve hot with cream or ice cream.

Serves 4 – 5

CRÊPES SUZETTE

The pancakes can be made ahead, cooked, then wrapped in foil and stored in the refrigerator for a couple of days or they may be kept in the freezer for a couple of months. Get all the ingredients for the sauce ready, then combine them in the pan just before serving and reheat the pancakes in the sauce one by one and arrange on a really hot serving dish and serve at once.

Pancakes:
    4 oz (100 g) plain flour
    Pinch salt
    1 egg
    1 tablespoon oil
    ½ pint (300 ml) milk
    Oil for frying

Sauce:
    Juice of 2 oranges
    4 oz (100 g) unsalted butter
    2 oz (50 g) caster sugar
    1 tablespoon orange liqueur
    3 tablespoons brandy

To make the pancakes: sift the flour and salt into a bowl. Blend the egg, oil and milk together and beat into the flour to make a fairly thin batter. Heat a very little oil in a 7-inch (17.5-cm) frying pan. Add about 2 tablespoons batter into the centre of the pan and tilt and rotate to spread out the batter. Cook for a minute, then turn over and cook on the other side for a further minute. Turn out and make nine more pancakes in the same way.

For the sauce: put the orange juice, butter and sugar in a large frying pan and heat gently until the sugar has dissolved, then simmer gently for about 5 minutes, until the

sauce is syrupy. Lay one pancake in the pan and coat with
the sauce, fold into four and move it to one side of the pan.
Repeat with the rest of the pancakes. Add the liqueur and
brandy, making sure that the pancakes are piping hot.
Light it with a match. Arrange on a piping hot serving dish
and serve at once.

Makes 10 pancakes

APPLE KUCHEN

A quick and easy pudding to make that all the family love.

  4 oz (100 g) plain flour
  1 oz (25 g) caster sugar
  1 egg, beaten
  ½ pint (300 ml) milk
  2 oz (50 g) butter, melted
  1 lb (450 g) cooking apples
  Granulated sugar

Heat the oven to 425°F, 220°C, gas no. 7 and butter
thoroughly a shallow 2-pint (good litre) oven-proof dish.

Put the flour in a bowl with the caster sugar and make a well
in the centre. Blend the egg, milk and melted butter
together and add to the flour. Beat well to make a smooth
batter. Turn into the dish.

Peel, core and roughly chop the apples and spread evenly
over the batter. Bake in the oven for about 45 to 50 minutes,
until the mixture is golden brown, crisp around the edge
and the apple is tender. Sprinkle thoroughly with granulated sugar and serve piping hot with thin cream.

Serves 6

CRISP FRUIT FRITTERS

The best fruit fritters to my mind are apple but you can use raw young rhubarb or slightly under-ripe bananas. Sometimes we have apple fritters for tea rather than as a pudding. Then I do them as large apple rings and dip them in caster sugar and cinnamon as they come out of the hot fat. I copied this idea from the Swiss who serve them hot with cream and hot chocolate at tea time.

  1 lb (450 g) cooking apples, young rhubarb or bananas
  Caster sugar
  4 oz (100 g) plain flour
  1 egg, separated
  ¼ pint (150 ml) milk
  Deep fat or oil for frying

Prepare the fruit; the manner depends on which type you are using. Peel, quarter and core the apples and cut into thick slices. Cut the rhubarb and bananas into 2-inch (5-cm) lengths. Sprinkle the cut fruit with caster sugar.

Sift the flour into a bowl, making a well in the centre. Blend the egg yolk with the milk and then add to the flour to make a smooth thick batter. Whisk the egg white until stiff and fold it into the batter.

Heat the fat or oil in a large pan, dip the fruit in the batter, one piece at a time, and then fry until golden brown. Drain on kitchen paper and serve at once with sugar and cream – or lemon juice if you do not have a sweet tooth.

Serves 4

FRENCH PANCAKES – SOMETIMES KNOWN AS SAUCER PANCAKES

When I was a child this was one our favourites. The pancakes were made on tough saucers that had long since lost the cups that went with them. You slip them off really well-buttered saucers when they are cooked and put a blob of strawberry jam in the middle and then fold them over and sprinkle them with sugar. I now make them in small stainless steel shallow bowls or sometimes on non-stick silicone paper, or even in large individual Yorkshire pudding tins.

    2 oz (50 g) butter
    2 oz (50 g) caster sugar
    2 oz (50 g) self-raising flour
    2 eggs
    ½ pint (300 ml) milk
    Jam and caster sugar

Heat the oven to 375°F, 190°C, gas no. 5 and well grease eight old saucers or line them with a circle of silicone paper and put to heat in the oven.

Cream the butter and sugar together until soft and beat in the eggs a little at a time and then blend in the flour. Heat the milk until hot but not boiling and stir it into the creamed mixture.

Divide the batter between the saucers and bake for about 20 minutes until well risen and golden brown. Place a blob of jam on the pancakes and fold them in half. Sprinkle them with sugar and serve piping hot.

Serves 4

Soufflés, mousses and omelettes

Rich yet light, these are among the most satisfying of summertime desserts. They are always popular at parties and are not as difficult to make as many people would have you believe.

It is impossible to freeze hot soufflés and soufflé omelettes. Cold soufflés, on the other hand, freeze very well but they should be kept in the freezer no longer than four weeks as they are inclined to sink slightly after that time. It is, however, best to freeze them in a dish – as you would for a mousse – rather than standing up grandly above a soufflé dish.

HOT CHOCOLATE SOUFFLÉ

If you can make a white sauce you can make a hot soufflé. They are not difficult but need a bit of care with the timing. It is essential to use the correct sized soufflé dish so that the soufflé rises above the dish. Measure the soufflé dish that you have by pouring measured water in it in order to give you the capacity. I then write the size on the bottom of the dish with a waterproof marker pen to remind me next time I am using it. If you are serving a soufflé for a supper party make the sauce base ahead of time, including the addition of the yolks and flavouring, then 40 minutes before baking and serving fold in the whisked egg whites, turn into the dish and bake.

4 oz (100 g) plain chocolate
2 tablespoons water
½ pint (300 ml) milk
1½ oz (40 g) butter
1½ oz (40 g) flour
¼ teaspoon vanilla essence
4 large eggs
2 oz (50 g) caster sugar
A little icing sugar

Heat the oven to 375°F, 190°C, gas no. 5 and place a baking sheet in it. Butter a 2-pint (a good litre) soufflé dish.

Break the chocolate into small pieces, put in a pan with the water and 2 tablespoons milk and stir over a low heat until the chocolate has melted, then add the remaining milk and bring to the boil. Remove the pan from the heat.

Melt the butter in a small pan, stir in the flour and cook for two minutes without browning. Remove from the heat and stir in the hot milk, return to the heat and bring to the boil, stirring until thickened, add vanilla essence and leave to cool.

Separate the eggs and beat the yolks one at a time into the chocolate sauce and then sprinkle on the sugar. Whisk the egg whites using a rotary hand or electric whisk until they are stiff but not dry. Stir one tablespoonful into the mixture and then carefully fold in the remainder. Pour into the dish, run a teaspoon around the edge and bake on a hot baking sheet in the centre of the oven for about 40 minutes. Sprinkle with icing sugar and serve at once with whipped cream.

Serves 4

VARIATIONS ON A HOT SOUFFLÉ

Choose any of the following flavourings instead of the chocolate and 2 tablespoons of water, and add to the mixture before the egg yolks.

Lemon
Add the finely grated rind of 2 small lemons and the juice of half a lemon to the mixture, leave out the vanilla essence and increase the caster sugar to 3 oz (75 g).

Orange
Add the finely grated rind of 2 small oranges and the juice of half an orange to the mixture, leave out the vanilla essence and increase the caster sugar to 3 oz (75 g).

Coffee
Add 2 tablespoons coffee essence to the milk and leave out the vanilla essence.

CHILLED SHARP LEMON SOUFFLÉ

This classic Milanaise soufflé is made in a soufflé dish – see notes about capacities of soufflés in the introduction to Hot Soufflés. A 3-inch (7.5-cm) band of greaseproof paper or foil is tied around the sides of the dish so that the dish is filled about 1½ inches (3.5 cm) above the dish (this will vary with the width of the dish). The paper is then removed, with the help of a knife dipped in boiling water, when the soufflé has set. The same mixture may be put in a glass dish and called a mousse.

2 large or 3 small lemons
1 packet or ½ oz (12½ g) gelatine
3 tablespoons water
3 eggs, separated
3 – 4 oz caster sugar (75 g – 100 g), use less if you like
   it very sharp
¼ pint (150 ml) whipping cream, whipped

To decorate:
2 oz (50 g) pistachio nuts or browned almonds
¼ pint (150 ml) whipping cream, whipped

Tie a double band of greaseproof paper 3 inches (7.5 cm) above the top of a 1-pint (600-ml) soufflé dish.

Finely grate the rind and squeeze and strain the juice from the lemons. Place the gelatine and water in a small bowl or cup. Stand for 3 minutes until it becomes a sponge, then stand the bowl in a pan of simmering water and allow the gelatine to dissolve. Keep it slightly warm.

Put the egg yolks, lemon juice and rind with the sugar in a large bowl and stand over a pan of simmering water and whisk until thick and creamy, this will take about 10 minutes. Remove from the heat and continue whisking until cool, then pour in the gelatine, whisking all the time until well blended.

Whisk the egg whites with an electric or hand rotary whisk until fairly stiff, then fold first the cream and then the egg whites into the lemon mixture until smoothly blended. Pour into the dish, smooth the top and leave to set, in a cool place. Untie the band of greaseproof paper and peel off with the help of a knife. Finely chop the nuts and press firmly into the sides of the soufflé. Decorate the top with swirls of whipped cream.

Serves 6

PINEAPPLE MOUSSE

An inexpensive mousse with a strong pineapple flavour.

    3 eggs, separated
    Juice of 1 lemon
    2 oz (50 g) caster sugar
    1 packet or ½ oz (12½ g) powdered gelatine
    ½ pint (300 ml) canned pineapple juice
    ¼ pint (150 ml) double cream

Put the egg yolks, lemon juice and sugar in a heat-proof bowl over a pan of simmering water and whisk until pale and thick. Remove from the heat and leave to cool, whisking occasionally.

Put the gelatine and 4 tablespoons of the pineapple juice in a small bowl and leave to stand for 5 minutes until it becomes a sponge. Place the bowl in a pan of simmering water and leave until dissolved, then add the remaining pineapple juice. Stir this into the egg yolk mixture. Leave in a cool place until just beginning to set, stirring frequently.

Whisk the cream until it is thick and fold into the pineapple mixture. Whisk the egg whites with an electric or rotary hand whisk until stiff and then fold into the mixture.

Turn into a glass serving dish and leave in the refrigerator for several hours to chill thoroughly. Serve decorated with a little extra cream piped into rosettes.

Serves 6

PINEAPPLE CHEESECAKE MOUSSE

There is no need to use first quality rings or chunks for this pudding, use crushed pineapple pieces instead.

3 eggs, separated
Grated rind and juice of 1 lemon
3 oz (75 g) caster sugar
4 level teaspoons gelatine
3 tablespoons water
$\frac{1}{2}$ lb (225 g) cream cheese
$13\frac{1}{4}$ oz (376 g) can crushed pineapple
$\frac{1}{4}$ pint (150 ml) double cream
Glacé pineapple to decorate

Place the egg yolks, lemon rind and juice with the sugar in a bowl. Stand over a pan of hot water and whisk until thick and creamy. Remove from the heat and continue whisking from time to time until cool.

Place the gelatine with the water in a small cup or bowl and leave to stand for 5 minutes until it becomes a sponge, then place in a pan of simmering water until the gelatine has dissolved and become clear. Cool slightly and stir into the egg yolk mixture.

Beat the cream cheese with the pineapple until thoroughly blended. Stir into the egg mixture and leave on one side until the mixture starts to thicken and set.

Whisk the cream until it forms soft peaks and whisk the egg whites until stiff and fold first the cream and then the egg whites into the pineapple mixture. Turn into a 3-pint glass (1.7-l) serving dish and leave in the refrigerator until set.

Decorate the top with pieces of glacé pineapple.

Serves 6 – 8

FRESH BLACKBERRY MOUSSE

This may be made from fresh or frozen blackberries – a tasty mousse that is a lovely red colour.

    1 lb (450 g) blackberries
    4 oz (100 g) caster sugar
    ½ oz (12½ g) gelatine
    4 tablespoons water
    ½ pint (300 ml) whipping cream

Lay the blackberries in a single layer on a large flat dish, sprinkle with sugar and leave for at least 3 hours to allow the juice to run out; then sieve them. When the blackberries are prepared like this it makes sieving very easy.

Put the gelatine and water in a cup or small bowl and leave to stand for 5 minutes until it becomes a sponge. Stand in a pan of simmering water until the gelatine has become clear, remove from the heat, cool slightly and stir into the blackberry purée. Leave it until the purée starts to thicken and set.

Whisk the cream until it forms soft peaks and then fold it into the purée. Turn into a 2-pint (1.1-l) glass serving dish and leave to set.

Serves 4 – 6

MIDNIGHT MOUSSE

This is a light inexpensive mousse. Add the rind of the lemons to the mousse too, making sure that it is very finely grated and including only the bright yellow zest.

1 lemon jelly
½ pint (300 ml) boiling water
Finely grated rind and juice of 2 large or 3 small
  lemons
4 eggs, separated
2 – 4 oz (50 g – 100 g) caster sugar

Mimosa balls
Angelica

Put the jelly, broken into small pieces, in a large bowl with the boiling water and stir until dissolved. Strain the lemon juice and stir into the jelly with the rind.

Beat the egg yolks with the caster sugar until creamy and stir into the jelly; leave in a cool place until starting to set.

Whisk the egg whites with an electric or hand rotary whisk until they are stiff and then fold into the lemon mixture. Turn into a 2½-pint (1.4-1) glass serving dish and leave to set.

Decorate with mimosa balls and small leaves of angelica.

Serves 6

APRICOT AND LEMON MOUSSE

Apricots are one of the best of the canned fruits to use as base for a mousse.

14½ -oz (411-g) can apricots
1 packet lemon jelly
Juice of ½ a lemon
½ pint (300 ml) whipping cream
A few thin slices of lemon

Strain the juice of the apricots into a measure and make up to ½ pint (300 ml) with water. Put in a saucepan with the jelly broken into small pieces and heat gently until dissolved. Remove from the heat, stir in the lemon juice and turn into a bowl. Leave on one side until just beginning to set.

Purée the apricots in a blender. Whisk the cream with an electric or rotary whisk until thick and forming soft peaks; remove a quarter of the cream and put on one side to use for decoration. Fold the remaining cream into the half-set jelly, together with the apricot purée. Turn into a 1¾-pint (1-l) glass serving dish and leave to set.

Spoon the remaining cream in blobs around the edge of the dish and place a twisted slice of lemon on top of each.

Serves 4 – 5

RICH CHOCOLATE MOUSSE

Very special and boozy. There is no need to use cream in this recipe, evaporated milk gives richness and the flavour is drowned by the real chocolate, orange and liqueur.

 ½ oz (12½ g) gelatine
 Grated rind and juice of 1 orange
 8 oz (225 g) plain chocolate
 4 eggs, separated
 2 tablespoons orange liqueur or brandy
 4 oz (100 g) caster sugar
 1 small can evaporated milk, chilled
 A little whipped cream to decorate

Soak the gelatine with the rind and juice of the orange in a small cup or basin and leave until it becomes a sponge. Then stand the cup in a pan of simmering water until it has completely dissolved and is runny.

Put another basin containing the chocolate broken into small pieces over the pan of hot water and leave until melted. Add the egg yolks, remove from the heat and stir until smooth.
Add the gelatine mixture to the chocolate mixture and liqueur. Stir well and leave for about 5 minutes until cool but not set.

Meanwhile whisk the egg whites, using a hand electric or rotary whisk, until they are frothy then add the sugar a teaspoonful at a time, whisking until it reaches a meringue consistency. Whisk the evaporated milk until it is thick and the whisk leaves a trail when lifted out. Quickly fold the chocolate mixture into the egg whites, then fold in the evaporated milk.

Turn into a 2½-pint (1.4-l) glass dish and chill until set. Decorate with swirls of whipped cream.

Serves 6 – 8

FRESH LIME MOUSSE

When limes are not in season, or are too expensive, use lemons. This mousse is very light and is not at all rich as it contains no cream.

    4 eggs
    4 oz (100 g) caster sugar
    2 large limes
    ½ oz (12½ g) gelatine
    3 tablespoons cold water
    Whipped cream and lime slices to decorate

Separate the eggs and place the yolks in a bowl with the sugar; beat well until blended and creamy. Put the whites in a bowl ready for whisking.

Grate the rind and squeeze the juice from the limes and add both to the yolk mixture.

Place the gelatine and water in a small bowl or cup. Stand for 3 minutes until it becomes a sponge, then stand the bowl in a pan of simmering water and allow the gelatine to dissolve. Cool slightly and add to the yolk and lime mixture. Leave to cool but not set.

Whisk the egg whites, using a rotary or electric whisk, until stiff, then fold into the lime mixture. Put into a 2-pint (a good litre) glass dish and chill for at least 4 hours to set.

Decorate with whipped cream and lime slices and serve at room temperature.

Serves 6

SOUFFLÉ OMELETTES

This is such an easy spur-of-the-moment pudding when time is short and, perhaps, there is not much in the larder! I make it to follow a salad supper when there are just the two of us. The lemon variation is sharp and delicious.

    2 large eggs
    1 dessertspoon caster sugar
    2 teaspoons cold water
    ½ oz (12½ g) butter
    1 rounded tablespoon black cherry or strawberry jam
    Icing sugar

Separate the eggs and place the yolks in a basin with the sugar and water; beat until pale and creamy. Whisk the egg whites, using a rotary or electric whisk, until they are just stiff. Mix 1 tablespoonful into the egg yolks and carefully fold in the remainder.

Heat an omelette pan and then melt the butter in it over a moderate heat. Spread the mixture into the pan and cook without moving for 3 to 4 minutes until a pale golden brown underneath.

Slip the pan under a medium grill for 2 to 3 minutes to set the top. Make a slight cut across the centre of the omelette;

spread one half with warmed jam, fold in half and slide onto a warm serving dish. Dredge with icing sugar and serve at once.

Serves 2

LEMON SOUFFLÉ OMELETTE

Add the rind and juice of half a lemon to the egg yolks and sugar and leave out the water, then make as above but do not fill with jam. Serve with lemon wedges and sprinkle with caster sugar.

Serves 2

HOT LEMON SOUFFLÉ PUDDING

This is one of my favourite lemon puddings. I have even, for one reason or another, baked it ahead of time and reheated it very satisfactorily in a meat tin of water for 30 minutes in a moderate oven. The top of the pudding is sponge mousse and the underneath a sharp lemon sauce.

   3 oz (75 g) butter or margarine, softened
   9 oz (250 g) caster sugar
   3 eggs, separated
   3 oz (75 g) self-raising flour
   Grated rind and juice of 2 lemons
   ¾ pint (450 ml) milk

Heat the oven to 375°F, 190°C, gas no. 5. Butter thoroughly a shallow 2½-pint (1.4-l) oven-proof dish.

Beat the butter or margarine with the sugar until smooth and beat in the egg yolks. Then stir in the flour, lemon rind, juice and milk. Do not worry if the mixture looks curdled at this stage – it is quite normal.

Whisk the egg whites using a hand rotary or electric whisk until they form soft peaks and then fold them into the lemon mixture. Pour into the prepared dish and place in a meat tin half filled with hot water. Bake for about 1 hour or until pale golden brown on top. The pudding will have a light sponge on top with its own sauce underneath.

Serves 4 – 6

Cheesecakes

Cheesecakes fall into two categories – those that have to be cooked and those with a gelatine base. Neither is difficult to do. Although a fruit-topping is deservedly popular there are some people who prefer their cheesecake plain.

Since they should always be frozen without a topping, an energetic cook can make and freeze several cheesecakes, removing two from the freezer and topping only one of them before serving. Always allow the cheesecake to thaw in the refrigerator before adding the topping. Toppings themselves can be frozen separately and thawed for use when necessary.

You will see in the uncooked cheesecake recipes that I make the cheesecake mixture then set it in the refrigerator. Then the biscuit crust is put on top of the cheesecake mixture and is returned to the refrigerator to firm up. Turn out by dipping the tin in a bowl or very hot water for a moment to release the cheesecake from the tin, then put a serving plate on top of the tin and reverse. Lift the tin off the cheesecake, peel off the circle of greaseproof paper and decorate the top as suggested in the recipe. This method means that you get a crisp base to the cheesecake and you do not need to buy a spring form tin.

ORANGE CHEESECAKE

This is a fresh tasting sharp cheesecake.

½ oz (12½ g) gelatine
3 tablespoons cold water
1 lb (450 g) rich cream cheese
6-oz (175-g) can frozen concentrated unsweetened
    orange juice, thawed
3 oz (75 g) caster sugar
½ pint (300 ml) whipping cream.
4 oz (100 g) digestive biscuits
2 oz (50 g) butter
1 oz (25 g) demerara sugar

Place the gelatine in a small basin with the cold water and leave to stand for 3 minutes. Then place it in a pan of simmering water and leave to dissolve until the gelatine has become clear; remove and leave to cool.

Cream the cheese until soft and gradually beat in the orange juice and caster sugar. Stir in the cooled gelatine. Whisk the cream until thick but not stiff and fold into the cheesecake mixture. Turn into a lightly oiled 8-inch (20-cm) cake tin, with a circle of greaseproof paper in the bottom, and place in the refrigerator.

Crush the biscuits finely. Melt the butter in a pan and stir in the biscuit crumbs and demerara sugar. Press this mixture over the cheesecake. Return to the refrigerator and leave for about 3 to 4 hours until the cheesecake is set and well chilled. Turn out onto a serving dish (see p. 73), remove greaseproof paper and decorate the top with whipped cream and fresh orange segments.

Serves 6 – 8

GRAPEFRUIT CHEESECAKE

This cheesecake is sharp, rich and creamy.

$\frac{1}{2}$ oz (12$\frac{1}{2}$ g) gelatine
3 tablespoons cold water
1 lb (450 g) rich cream cheese
6-oz (175-g) can frozen concentrated unsweetened
    grapefruit juice, thawed
3 oz (75 g) caster sugar
$\frac{1}{2}$ pint (300 ml) whipping cream
4 oz (100 g) digestive biscuits
2 oz (50 g) butter
1 oz (25 g) demerara sugar
Black and white grapes

Place the gelatine in a small basin with the cold water and leave to stand for 3 minutes. Then place it in a pan of simmering water and leave to dissolve until the gelatine has become clear; remove and leave it to cool.

Cream the cheese until soft and gradually beat in the grapefruit juice and caster sugar. Stir in the cooled gelatine. Whisk the cream until it is thick but not stiff and fold into the cheesecake mixture. Turn into a lightly oiled 8-inch

(20-cm) cake tin with a circle of greaseproof paper in the bottom. Place in the refrigerator.

Crush the biscuits finely. Melt the butter in a pan and stir in the biscuit crumbs and demerara sugar. Press this mixture over the cheesecake. Leave in the refrigerator for several hours.

Turn out onto a serving plate (see p. 73) and remove the greaseproof paper. Decorate the top with halved black and white grapes.

Serves 8

BLACK CHERRY AND ALMOND CHEESECAKE

If you are in a hurry use a can of black cherry pie filling for the topping, with a little liqueur, such as Kirsch, added.

> 6 digestive biscuits, crushed
> 1½ oz (40 g) butter melted
> 3 eggs, separated
> 4 oz (100 g) caster sugar
> 1 lb (450 g) cream cheese at room temperature
> ½ teaspoon vanilla essence
> A few flaked almonds
> 15-oz (425-g) can black cherries, preferably stoned
> 1 rounded teaspoon arrowroot

Heat the oven to 350°F, 180°C, gas no. 4. Lightly butter and flour a 7-inch (17.5-cm) round cake tin with a loose bottom.

Blend the biscuits with the melted butter and press firmly over the base of the cake tin.

Whisk the egg yolks and sugar until light and creamy and

stir in the cream cheese and vanilla essence until well blended. Whisk the egg whites, using a hand rotary or electric whisk, until they are stiff, fold into the cheese mixture and spoon into the tin. Sprinkle the almonds around the edge of the cheesecake.

Bake in the oven for about 1½ hours, until well risen, and pale golden brown and shrinking slightly away from the sides of the tin, then turn off the heat and leave in the oven for a further 15 to 30 minutes.

Remove from the oven and leave to cool in the tin until quite cold; this cheesecake will sink slightly in the centre on cooling. Remove from the tin and place on a serving dish. Drain the cherries and, if necessary, stone them. Reserve the juice and blend ¼ pint (150 ml) with the arrowroot in a small saucepan and then slowly bring to the boil, stirring until thickened. Add the cherries and mix lightly; spoon over the cheesecake and leave to cool completely. Chill before serving.

Serves 6 – 8

RHUBARB AND GINGER CHEESECAKE

Use young rhubarb for this recipe otherwise the colour and flavour will not be so good.

    1 lb (450 g) young rhubarb
    1 tablespoon ginger syrup
    4 oz (100 g) caster sugar
    3 tablespoons water
    ½ oz (12½ g) gelatine
    8 oz (225 g) rich cream cheese
    ¼ pint (150 ml) soured cream

2 eggs, separated
2 oz (50 g) butter
2 oz (50 g) ginger biscuits
2 oz (50 g) digestive biscuits

Line an 8-inch (20-cm) cake tin with a circle of greaseproof paper. Cut the rhubarb into short lengths and place in a saucepan with the ginger syrup and sugar. Place the saucepan over a low heat and simmer until the rhubarb is soft, stirring occasionally; this will take about 10 to 15 minutes.

Put the water in a small bowl or cup and sprinkle over the gelatine; leave to soak for 5 minutes. Take the fruit from the heat and stir in the soaked gelatine until it has dissolved. Put in a blender or sieve to make a purée, turn into a bowl and leave to cool, stirring occasionally until the mixture starts to set.

Cream the cheese and soured cream together and beat in the egg yolks. Then stir in the rhubarb purée. Whisk the egg whites with a hand rotary or electric whisk until they are stiff and then fold them into the mixture. Turn into the tin and chill in the refrigerator for an hour or until set.

Melt the butter in a small pan, finely crush the biscuits and stir into the melted butter. Spread over the cheesecake and return to the refrigerator to chill for a further hour.

Turn out onto a serving dish and, if liked, decorate with swirls of cream and small pieces of stem ginger.

Serves 8

Meringues and Pavlovas

There are a vast number of variations on a meringue theme and unfortunately I only have room to include a few. Like pastries, they are very versatile and can be served for tea as well as for pudding. Make tiny meringues for children's parties, adding vegetable colouring for instant decoration, and sandwich them together with teaspoonsfuls of whipped cream. Large meringue cases can be filled with fresh fruit in season, such as strawberries, sprinkled with sugar and piled high with cream.

There is no point in freezing ordinary meringues and meringue cases. They keep perfectly well in an airtight tin. Pavlovas should be frozen without their filling.

MERINGUES

My aim has never been to make snowy white meringues. I like them to be just off-white. I rarely pipe them as I prefer a non-shop looking finish. I spoon them onto the non-stick paper using two dessert spoons. Non-stick silicone paper is a must for meringues, far better than an oiled baking tray! Buy non-stick paper at any good stationers, either by the sheet or in a roll. You can use it over and over again for any sugary things that are likely to stick; after use just shake off the surplus sugar, put in a bag and keep for the next time. You can draw circles on the paper for a guide when making large meringue cases; I do pipe these as it is easier to get a more uniform shape.

Make the meringues by the method here and I guarantee success. Slowly add the sugar, beating with maximum force, and then cook very slowly. If you like meringues with squidgy centres cook for slightly less time.

To make 12 double meringues:
  4 egg whites
  8 oz (225 g) caster sugar
  Whipping cream

Heat the oven to 200°F, 100°C, and gas no. ¼ or Low and line two baking sheets with silicone paper.

Place the egg whites in a large bowl and whisk on high speed with an electric or hand rotary whisk until they form soft peaks. Add the sugar a teaspoonful at a time, whisking well after each addition, until all the sugar has been added. Using 2 dessertspoons, spoon the meringue out onto the baking sheets, putting 12 meringues on each tray.

Bake in the oven for 3 to 4 hours until the meringues are firm and dry and will lift easily from the silicone paper. They will be a very pale off-white or slightly darker if you have used soft brown sugar. Whisk the cream until thick and use to sandwich the meringue shells together.

BROWN MERINGUES

Make exactly as above but use 8 oz (225 g) light soft brown sugar.

CELEBRATION FRUIT MERINGUE

3 egg whites
6 oz (175 g) caster sugar

Filling:
½ pint (300 ml) double cream
3 tablespoons cointreau
4 oz (100 g) raspberries
1 peach
Juice of one small orange
1 kiwi fruit, peeled and sliced
Sprig of fresh mint

Heat the oven to 200°F, 100°C, gas no ¼ or Low. Line a baking sheet with silicone paper. Mark a circle on it of 8 inches (20 cm), using a flan or cake tin or plate.

Place the egg whites in a large bowl and whisk on high speed with an electric or hand rotary whisk until they form soft peaks. Add the sugar a teaspoonful at a time, whisking well after each addition until all the sugar has been added.

Place the meringue in a piping bag, fitted with a large rose pipe and fill the circle to make a flat base. Pipe rosettes of meringue around the edge to build up the sides.

Bake in the oven for 3 to 4 hours until the meringue is crisp and has dried out. Remove from the oven and leave to cool. Place on serving dish.

Put the double cream and cointreau in a basin and whisk until thick and the mixture forms soft peaks; spoon into the centre of the meringue basket and arrange the raspberries in a circle around the edge of the cream.

Peel and quarter the peach and cut into slices and dip in a little orange juice to prevent discolouration. Arrange in the centre of the cream with alternate slices of kiwi fruit and decorate with a sprig of mint in the centre.

Serves 6

MERINGUE LAYERS

4 eggs whites
8 oz (225 g) caster sugar *or*
4 oz (100 g) caster sugar and 4 oz (100 g) light soft
   brown sugar.

Heat the oven to 200°F, 100°C, gas no. ¼ or Low.

Line two large baking sheets with non-stick silicone paper. On one baking tray mark out a circle 8 inches (20 cm) in diameter. On the other baking tray mark one circle 7 inches (17.5 cm) and another circle 6 inches (15 cm) in diameter; use plates and saucers as guides.

Place the egg whites in a large bowl and whisk on high speed with an electric or hand rotary whisk until they form soft peaks. Add the sugar a teaspoonful at a time whisking well after each addition. (If using caster and light brown sugar it is important to sieve them together two or three times in order to mix them thoroughly before starting to whisk into the egg whites.) Continue whisking well after each addition until all the sugar has been added.

Divide the meringue between the marked circles and spread it out evenly to cover. Bake in the oven for 3 to 4 hours, until the meringues are firm to touch and dried out. Remove from the oven, leave to cool and peel off the paper.

The meringue layers may be filled with a mixture of fruit and cream. Soft fruit such as raspeberries or strawberries make a good filling if mixed with ½ pint (300 ml) whipped whipping cream. Spread half the filling on the largest piece of meringue, then cover with the next size of meringue, spread over the remaining cream and place the smallest meringue layer on top. Place on a serving dish and leave to stand for at least an hour before serving.

GINGER AND PINEAPPLE MERINGUE LAYER

Thoroughly drain an 8¾-oz (248-g) can of crushed pineapple and stir it into ½ pint (300 ml) whipped whipping cream together with 2 to 3 pieces of stem ginger finely chopped. Layer as above.

Serves 6 – 8

CHOCOLATE MERINGUE GÂTEAU

This is an impressive gâteau; make it for a special occasion or dinner party. It improves with keeping so make it a day before it is required.

3 egg whites
3 oz (75 g) caster sugar
3 oz (75 g) light soft brown sugar

Chocolate filling:
¼ pint (150 ml) milk
2 oz (50 g) caster sugar
2 oz (50 g) plain chocolate
3 egg yolks
1 level teaspoon cornflour
6 oz (175 g) unsalted butter, softened

Topping:
¼ pint (150 ml) whipping cream, whipped
12 Maltesers

Heat the oven to 300°F, 150°C, gas no. 2 and line two large baking sheets with non-stick silicone paper.

Put the egg whites in a large bowl and whisk with a hand rotary or an electric whisk on high speed until they are stiff. Sieve the two sugars together two or three times until well blended and then whisk into the egg whites a spoonful at a time. Spread the meringue in two circles 8 inches (20 cm) in diameter on the baking sheets and bake for 1 hour in the oven. Then turn off the heat and leave in the oven to cool.

Chocolate filling: first make the chocolate custard sauce. Put the milk, sugar and chocolate, broken into small pieces, in a basin and place over a pan of hot water. Heat gently until the chocolate has melted and blended with the milk. Stir a little of the hot liquid onto the egg yolks, which have been blended with the cornflour, and then add to the remaining chocolate mixture and stir until thickened. This will take about 5 to 10 minutes and the sauce is ready when it will coat the back of the spoon. Remove from the heat and leave to become quite cold.

Cream the butter and beat in the chocolate sauce. If by any chance the butter cream should curdle because the butter and chocolate custard are not at the same termperature, warm the bowl slightly by standing in hot water and then beat well.

Place one meringue circle on a serving dish and spread with half of the chocolate cream, then cover with other meringue layer. Spread the rest of the chocolate cream on top and mark attractively with a palette knife.

Pipe the whipped cream in 12 large rosettes around the edge of the gateau and press a Malteser into the centre of each rosette. Keep in the refrigerator until required and then allow to stand at room temperature for 2 to 3 hours before serving.

Serves 6

SWISS HAZELNUT MERINGUE WITH CHESTNUTS

Meringue and hazelnuts go well together. Look out for flaked hazelnuts; they are far cheaper than flaked almonds. Our local delicatessen sells them, and so do large stores such as Selfridges.

    4 oz (100 g) hazelnuts
    4 egg whites
    8 oz (225 g) caster sugar

  1 teaspoon white vinegar
  $\frac{1}{2}$ oz (12$\frac{1}{2}$ g) flaked hazelnuts

Filling:
  $\frac{1}{4}$ pint (150 ml) double cream
  2 tablespoons brandy
  8-oz (235-g) can sweetened chestnut purée

Heat the oven to 350°F, 180°C, gas no. 4. Lightly brush the sides of two 8-inch (20-cm) sandwich tins with oil and line the base with silicone non-stick paper.

Place the whole hazelnuts on a tray and put in the oven for about 5 to 6 minutes, then tip onto a clean tea towel and rub them well together to remove all the skins. Place in an electric blender and grind.

Whisk the egg whites on maximum speed with an electric or hand rotary whisk until they are stiff and then whisk in half the sugar, a teaspoonful at a time. Mix the ground hazel nuts with the remaining sugar and carefully fold into the egg whites with the vinegar.

Divide the mixture between the two sandwich tins and spread flat. Sprinkle the flaked hazelnuts on top of the mixture in one of the tins. Bake in the oven for 45 minutes then turn off the heat and leave to cool in the oven. Then remove from the oven and turn out of the tins; remove the paper.

Put the meringue with the hazelnuts on top on one side and place the other on a serving dish.

Lightly whisk the cream with the brandy until thick. Spread the chestnut purée over the meringue on the serving dish and then cover with the whipped brandy cream. Place the second meringue on top and leave to stand for at least 4 hours before serving.

Serves 8

MARGARET'S PAVLOVA

This is one of my sister-in-law's specialities – and rather good it is too!

    3 egg whites
    6 oz (175 g) caster sugar
    1 teaspoon vinegar
    1 level teaspoon cornflour

Filling:
    Grated rind and juice of 2 lemons
    1 oz (25 g) cornflour
    4 oz (100 g) caster sugar
    3 egg yolks
    ¼ pint (150 ml) soured or double cream

Lay a sheet of silicone paper on a baking tray and mark an 8-inch (20-cm) circle on it. Heat the oven to 325°F, 160°C, gas no. 3.

Whisk the egg whites with an electric or rotary hand whisk until they are stiff, then whisk in almost all the sugar, a spoonful at a time. Blend the vinegar with the cornflour and whisk into the egg whites with the last spoonful of sugar. Spread the meringue out to cover the circle on the baking tray, building up the sides to come higher than the centre.

Put the baking tray in the oven and then turn down the heat to 300°F, 150°C, gas no. 2 and bake for 1 hour; then turn off the oven and leave the Pavlova to become quite cold in the oven.

Now prepare the filling: put the lemon rind and juice in a measure and make up to ½ pint (300 ml) with cold water. Put the cornflour and sugar in a small bowl and stir in the lemon mixture, pour into a saucepan and bring to the boil, stirring until it thickens. Add the egg yolks, remove from the heat and stir until well blended. Leave to cool. Lightly whip the cream until it just forms soft peaks and fold it into the lemon mixture.

Place the Pavlova on a serving dish and spoon the filling into the centre. Leave to stand for an hour in the refrigerator before serving.

Serves 6 – 8

PAVLOVA WITH KIWI FRUIT

This is very like meringue, but the middle is lovely and soft.

   3 egg whites
   6 oz (175 g) caster sugar
   1 teaspoon vinegar
   1 level teaspoon cornflour
   ½ pint (300 ml) whipped whipping cream
   A little cointreau and fresh orange juice
   1 Kiwi fruit

Lay a sheet of silicone non-stick paper on a baking tray and mark an 8-inch (20-cm) circle on it. Heat the oven to 325°F, 160°C, gas no. 3.

Whisk the egg whites with an electric or rotary hand whisk until they are stiff, then whisk in the sugar a teaspoonful at a time. Blend the vinegar with the cornflour and whisk into the egg whites with the last spoonful of sugar.

Spread the meringue out to cover the circle on the baking tray, building up the sides to come higher than the centre. Put in the oven and turn the heat down to 300°F, 150°C, gas no. 2 and bake for one hour. The Pavlova will be a pale creamy colour rather than snowy white. Turn off the oven and leave to become quite cold in the oven.

Remove from the baking tray and place on a serving dish. Flavour the cream with a little cointreau and fresh orange juice to taste and pile into the centre of the Pavlova. Leave it to stand in the refrigerator for one hour before serving.

Slice the Kiwi fruit and arrange around the edge of the Pavlova.

Serves 6 – 8

FUN PUDDING

This is adapted from an old recipe from the first principal of the City of Bath College of Home Economics – where I was trained. It is a baked custard with apple and meringue.

1 lb (450 g) cooking apples
2 level tablespoons caster sugar
Grated rind of 1 lemon
1 level tablespoon arrowroot
$\frac{1}{2}$ pint (300 ml) milk
$\frac{1}{4}$ pint (150 ml) double cream
$1\frac{1}{2}$ oz (40 g) caster sugar
2 egg yolks

Meringue:
2 egg whites
2 oz (50 g) caster sugar

Heat the oven to 325°F, 160°C, gas no. 3.

Peel, core and very thinly slice the apples and place in a 2-pint (a good litre) pie dish, sprinkle with 2 tablespoons caster sugar and the grated rind of a lemon.

Blend the arrowroot with a little of the milk. Then bring the remainder of the milk to the boil and stir it into the arrowroot. Return the mixture to the pan and bring to the boil, stirring until thickened, then remove from the heat and stir in the cream and caster sugar and egg yolks, blended together. Pour over the apples.

Whisk the egg whites with a rotary or electric hand whisk and, when the egg whites are stiff, whisk in the sugar a teaspoonful at a time. Spread over the custard, right to the edges of the dish.

Bake in the oven for about 45 minutes to 1 hour or until the meringue is pale brown, the custard set and the apples tender.

Serves 6

PINEAPPLE MERINGUE PUDDING

This is an out of the ordinary pudding for a family meal. It is useful if you can slip it into the oven when a casserole is cooking and the oven is on low.

   1½ oz (40 g) butter
   1½ oz (40 g) flour
   8-oz (225-g) can pineapple pieces
   2 large eggs, separated
   5 oz (150 g) caster sugar

Heat the oven to 300°F, 150°C, gas no. 2 and well butter a 1½-pint (900-ml) pie dish.

Melt the butter in a saucepan and stir in the flour and cook for 1 minute. Drain the juice from the can of pineapple and make up to ½ pint (300 ml) with water, add to the pan and bring to the boil, stirring until thickened. Remove from the heat and stir in the egg yolks and 2 oz (50 g) caster sugar, then fold in the pineapple pieces and put into the dish.

Whisk the egg whites until stiff then whisk in the remaining sugar a spoonful at a time. Pile onto the pineapple mixture and bake in the oven for 30 to 40 minutes until the meringue is crisp and a pale golden brown. Serve hot.

Serves 4

Milk puddings, yogurt and old-fashioned junket

These are nursery fare, often more popular with grown-ups than with children. Children have a horrible habit of turning up their noses at classical milk puddings and old-fashioned junket – they suspect that it might be good for them! Persuade them to taste a little of the home-made kind and they should be converts in an instance.

Most of the recipes that follow cannot be frozen as they separate when they thaw. Home-made yogurt is not suitable for the freezer either. Caramel custard keeps well for up to three days in the refrigerator and, in fact, often improves in the waiting.

CUSTARDS

Real egg custards have never been my forte; I now always add some cornflour and get an excellent consistency. Make it carefully, watching all the time; without a double saucepan it needs constant stirring.

POURING CUSTARD

3 eggs (or 2 whole eggs and 1 yolk)
1 oz (25 g) caster sugar
1 teaspoon cornflour
1 pint (600 ml) milk

Beat the eggs with the sugar and cornflour until smooth. Heat the milk to quite hot, but do not boil, and gradually stir it into the eggs. Pour back into the saucepan and stir over a gentle heat continuously until it is creamy and will coat the back of the spoon. Strain into a cold bowl so that cooking stops immediately. If it is to be used later, cover with a piece of damp greaseproof paper to stop a skin forming.

THICKER CUSTARD (for Trifles)

3 egg yolks
1 oz (25 g) caster sugar
1 heaped teaspoon cornflour
½ pint (300 ml) milk

Mix together the egg yolks, sugar and cornflour. Warm the milk in a pan until hand-hot and pour it onto the egg yolks, stirring constantly. Return the mixture to the saucepan and cook gently, stirring until it thickens. Do not allow it to boil or the custard will curdle. Cool and then use in a trifle.

BAKED CUSTARD

4 eggs (or 2 whole eggs and 2 yolks)
1 oz (25 g) caster sugar
1 pint (600 ml) milk

Heat the oven to 325°F, 160°C, gas no. 3.

Beat the eggs with the sugar until creamy. Heat the milk to quite hot and gradually stir it into the eggs. Strain into a buttered dish and stand in a baking tin with warm water coming half way up the sides. If liked sprinkle with a little nutmeg and bake in the oven for 1 to 1½ hours until set, or until a knife inserted in the middle comes out clean. Serve either hot or cold.

JUNKET

Pasteurized milk is the kind that the milkman usually delivers; if you want a richer junket use Channel Island milk. Leave the junket to set in a warm kitchen and do not chill until it is set.

   1 pint (600 ml) pasteurized or Channel Island milk
   2 level teaspoons caster sugar
   1 teaspoon essence of rennet

Put the milk and sugar in a saucepan and warm to blood heat. The temperature should be no more than 98°F (37°C); to test, dip the tip of the little finger in the milk. It should strike neither hot or cold, but should feel comfortably warm.

Pour the milk into a serving dish and stir in the rennet. Leave undisturbed for 1½ to 2 hours until the junket has set. Then transfer to the refrigerator and chill thoroughly and serve very cold.

Serves 4

BAKED RICE PUDDING

My family adore rice pudding. I make double the quantity as they are always starving and make it with diluted evaporated milk. I use a large can and make it up to 1¾ pint (1-l) with water and then just add ¼ pint (150 ml) ordinary milk. The result is very rich and creamy.

2 oz (50 g) pudding rice
1 pint (600 ml) milk
1 oz (25 g) caster sugar
1 strip of lemon peel
A little grated nutmeg, optional
$\frac{1}{2}$ oz ($12\frac{1}{2}$ g) butter.

Wash the rice and drain well. Put into a $1\frac{1}{2}$-pint (900-ml) buttered oven-proof dish and stir in the milk. Leave for about 30 minutes for the rice to soften. Add the sugar and lemon peel and stir well. Sprinkle the top with nutmeg and dot with butter.

Bake in the centre of a cool oven, 300°F, 150°C, gas no. 2 for 2 to $2\frac{1}{2}$ hours. The skin may be stirred in two or three times during the first hour of cooking to increase the creaminess.

Serves 4

To make a richer rice pudding:
Remove the pudding from the oven after $1\frac{1}{2}$ or 2 hours and cool for 10 minutes, then stir in a well beaten egg and return to the oven and bake for a further $\frac{1}{2}$ to 1 hour.

BAKED TAPIOCA PUDDING

Follow the recipe for rice pudding but instead of the rice use 2 oz (50 g) washed tapioca.

BAKED MACARONI PUDDING

Follow the recipe for rice pudding but instead of rice use 2 oz (50 g) broken and washed macaroni.

HOME-MADE YOGURT

Home-made yogurt is far cheaper than bought. Adding milk powder gives a firmer set.

 1 pint (600 ml) milk
 1 tablespoon bought yogurt
 1 heaped tablespoon dried milk powder

Heat the milk to boiling, then cool in a bowl of cold water to about 112°F, 44°C – hot bath temperature. Put the yogurt in a bowl with the milk and whisk in the dried milk powder. Cover and put it either in a linen cupboard overnight or in a vacuum flask for 6 hours. Or, if you have one, use a yogurt making kit.

APRICOT YOGURT FOOL

 4 oz (100 g) dried apricots
 ½ pint (300 ml) boiling water
 4 oz (100 g) sugar
 ¾ pint (450 ml) plain yogurt

Soak the apricots overnight in ½ pint (300 ml) boiling water. Simmer with the sugar until tender, then purée in a blender or sieve and stir into the yogurt. Pour into a serving dish and chill thoroughly before serving.

Serves 4

PASSION PUDDING

This dish is one of my stand-bys and no one guesses it is just yogurt and cream with brown sugar. This is a good way of using home-made yogurt and making it special. For every day use ⅓ cream to ⅔ yogurt.

    ½ pint (300 ml) whipping cream
    ½ pint (300 ml) plain yogurt
    Dark soft brown sugar

Lightly whip the cream and blend with the yogurt. Put the mixture in a 1¼-pint (750-ml) glass dish or four individual glasses. Sprinkle the top with a ¼-inch layer of sugar. Leave overnight in the refrigerator. Sprinkle again with more sugar before serving well chilled.

Serves 4

CRÈME CARAMEL

The secret of making crème caramel is to cook it slowly so that the custard does not boil and make the crème tough and full of holes. If preferred make individual crème caramels in remekin dishes or cups without handles.

Caramel:
    3 oz (75 g) granulated sugar
    3 tablespoons water

Crème:
    5 eggs
    2 oz (50 g) caster sugar
    A few drops of vanilla essence
    1¼ pint (750 ml) milk

Heat the oven to 300°F, 150°C, gas no. 2.

To make the caramel: put the sugar and water in a heavy saucepan and dissolve the sugar over a low heat. Bring to the boil and boil until the syrup is a pale golden brown. Remove from the heat and quickly pour the caramel into a 1¾-pint (1-l) charlotte mould, cake tin or soufflé dish.

For the crème; mix together the eggs, sugar and vanilla essence. Warm the milk in a saucepan over a low heat until it is handhot, then pour it onto the egg mixture, stirring constantly.

Butter the sides of the tin or mould above the caramel. Strain the custard into the tin or mould and place in a roasting tin half filled with hot water. Bake in the oven for 1½ hours or until a knife inserted in the centre comes out clean. Do not worry if it takes longer than the time given to cook; it will set eventually. Do not increase the oven temperature or the custard will have bubbles in it.

Remove from the oven and leave to cool completely for at least 12 hours or overnight. Turn out carefully onto a flat serving dish that is sufficiently deep to catch the caramel juices.

Serves 6

NORWEGIAN CREAM

A classic Cordon Bleu recipe; very good but no one from Norway has heard of it!

6 oz (175 g) apricot jam
3 large eggs
1 level tablespoon caster sugar
¾ pint (450 ml) milk
A little vanilla essence
2 oz (50 g) plain chocolate
½ pint (300 ml) double cream, whipped

Heat the oven to 325°F, 160°C, gas no. 3 and spread the jam in the base of a 2-pint (a good litre) dish.

Whisk two whole eggs and one egg yolk in a small bowl with the sugar. Heat the milk until just warm, but do not boil. Pour it onto the egg mixture and add a little vanilla essence to taste. Strain into the dish on top of the jam. Cover with a lid of foil and stand in a baking tin half filled with hot water and bake in the oven for 1¾ hours or until the custard is set. Lift out the dish and leave to cool, then chill overnight in the refrigerator.

Coarsely grate the chocolate and sprinkle half over the custard. Whisk the egg white until stiff and then fold into half the cream and spread over the custard so that the chocolate is completely hidden.

Put the remaining cream into a piping bag fitted with a large rose pipe and pipe the cream around the edge of the dish. Sprinkle with the rest of the chocolate and serve.

Serves 6

Special cream puddings and cheats

These really are special cream puddings; extremely rich, rather boozy and very, very good. Make them for special parties, particulary when your guests are gluttons. Finicky feeders are better off with fruit salad (see next chaper). These are for jolly gutsy people who like to taste the alcohol and can't resist dipping their fingers in the cream – people, in fact, who scrape their plates clean and ask for more!

Do not try and freeze any of these puddings, except the Brandy and Chocolate Layer and the Chocolate Roulade. In any case, they are mainly quick and easy to make and you won't have any left overs.

CHOCOLATE BEACON

Chocolate Beacon is one of those easy cold puddings that tastes super and very rich. Sometimes I make it in straight sided stemmed glasses; the layers look attractive in white and chocolate. Serve very cold. You can be even more generous with the cream for special occasions.

    4 rounded tablespoons drinking chocolate
    1 level tablespoon coffee powder
    4 oz (100 g) fresh brown breadcrumbs
    4 oz (100 g) demerara sugar
    ½ pint (300 ml) whipping cream
    A little grated chocolate

Place the chocolate, coffee powder, breadcrumbs and sugar together in a bowl and mix thoroughly.

Whisk the cream with a rotary or electric hand whisk until it is thick and soft peaks are formed.

Starting with the chocolate mixture, layer with the whipped cream in a serving dish, finishing with a layer of cream. Leave in a cool place for at least 8 to 10 hours before serving.

This pudding may be made a day in advance. Before serving decorate with a little grated chocolate.

Serves 4

CHOCOLATE ROULADE

A touch of the Cordon Bleu and very good too. If you do not have a large Swiss roll tin make a paper case about 13 inches × 9 inches (33 cm × 22 cm) from two sheets of well-greased greaseproof or silicone paper, fold at each corner and secure with paper clips or staple the corners. Put this case on a thick baking sheet.

  6 oz (185 g) plain chocolate
  5 eggs, separated
  6 oz (185 g) caster sugar
  3 tablespoons hot water
  ½ pint (300 ml) whipping cream
  Icing sugar, sieved

Heat the oven to 350°F, 180°C, gas no. 4. Line a greased Swiss roll tin about 13½ inches × 9½ inches (34 cm × 24 cm) with greased greaseproof paper.

First melt the chocolate slowly in a bowl that is standing over a pan of hot, not simmering, water. Whisk the egg yolks and caster sugar together until light in colour and texture, using a balloon or electric whisk. Stir the hot water into the melted chocolate and then mix with the egg yolk mixture. Whisk the egg whites with the electric or rotary whisk until light and firm and then carefully fold into the chocolate mixture until no white specks remain. Pour evenly into the tin and bake for 12 to 18 minutes; when cooked the sponge mixture will be firm to the touch.

Remove from the oven, leave in the tin and cover, without touching the roulade, with a piece of greaseproof paper and a tea cloth that has been rung out in warm water. Place in a cold larder or refrigerator for 12 hours or overnight. Covering the roulade with a damp teacloth prevents a hard crust forming.

Whip the cream with an electric or rotary whisk until it will just hold its shape. Dust a large piece of greaseproof paper with icing sugar, turn out the roulade and peel off the lining paper. Spread with the cream and roll up like a Swiss roll, using the paper to help. Expect the roll to crack a bit, like the bark of a tree, this is all part of its charm! Dust generously with icing sugar and place on a serving dish.

Serves 6 – 8

BRANDY AND CHOCOLATE LAYER

A really luxurious looking rich chocolate pudding. Serve thin slices. You certainly do not need to use butter for this recipe as the flavour would not come through. As you cut slices through the cake the brandy soaked biscuits show in a definite layer. It looks as if you have been busy baking all morning – rather a cheat of a pudding as it is made in ten minutes. You can freeze the loaf shape wrapped in foil, then thaw for six hours and decorate.

8 oz (225 g) margarine
7-oz (200-g) bar plain chocolate
2 eggs
1 oz (25 g) caster sugar
1 packet, 5½ oz (160 g), Nice biscuits
About 4 tablespoons brandy or, if you have not got
    any, use rum
¼ pint (150 ml) double cream, whipped
Chocolate buttons

Line a small loaf tin 7½ inches × 4 inches × 2½ inches (19 cm × 10 cm × 6 cm) with foil.

Put the margarine and chocolate, broken into small pieces, in a small saucepan and heat gently until melted.

Beat the eggs and sugar together until blended, then gradually add the chocolate mixture a little at a time, beating well. Pour about a third of this mixture into the tin.

Quickly dip the biscuits in the brandy and arrange them on top of the chocolate, close together, but not over-lapping, and sugar side down. Pour over another layer of chocolate, then arrange another layer of biscuites. Continue until the tin is full and all the biscuits have been used, finish with a layer of chocolate.

Chill in the refrigerator for at least 8 hours until firm and solid. Turn out into a serving dish and peel off the foil. Decorate with cream and chocolate buttons.

Serves 8 – 10

WALNUT COFFEE LAYER

Another of those easy cheat puddings; a great favourite with coffee addicts.

    1 oz (25 g) cocoa
    3 tablespoons boiling water
    3 oz (75 g) soft margarine
    3 oz (75 g) caster sugar
    2 oz (50 g) walnuts, chopped
    3 level teaspoons instant coffee
    ¼ pint boiling water
    4 tablespoons sherry
    1 packet (8) trifle sponge cakes
    ½ pint (300 ml) double cream
    A few whole walnuts to decorate

Cut a double thickness of greaseproof paper to fit the length of a 1-lb (450-g) loaf tin with the ends hanging over at each end. Lightly grease both the tin and the paper.

Put the cocoa in a bowl with the boiling water and stir until smooth and blended. Add the margarine and sugar and beat well until smooth and creamy. Stir in the chopped walnuts.

Dissolve the coffee in the boiling water and stir in the sherry. Dip four of the sponge cakes into the coffee and then lay side by side in the base of the tin. Spread the chocolate and walnut mixture over the sponge cakes and then cover with the remaining sponge cakes dipped in the coffee. Leave for at least 8 hours in the refrigerator or overnight. Lift out of the tin and place on a serving dish, removing the greaseproof paper.

Whisk the cream until thick and a soft piping consistency. Spread a layer of cream over the top and sides. Put the remaining cream into a piping bag fitted with a star pipe and pipe a border of cream around the base and rosettes on the top. Decorate with a few whole walnuts.

Serves 6 – 8

WHISKY CHOCOLATE GUNGE

Very quick, very easy and very good!

- 16 sponge finger biscuits
- 5 tablespoons strong black coffee
- 3 tablespoons whisky
- 7 oz (200 g) plain chocolate
- 4 eggs, separated
- A little whipped cream
- 1 oz (25 g) browned flaked almonds

Lay the sponge fingers in a single layer in a shallow 2-pint (a good litre) serving dish.

Blend the coffee and whisky together and pour over the sponge fingers. Leave to stand for 5 to 10 minutes until the fingers have soaked up the coffee mixture.

Break the chocolate into small pieces, place in a bowl and melt over a gentle heat over a pan of simmering water. Remove from the heat and beat in the egg yolks.

Whisk the egg whites with an electric or hand rotary whisk until they are stiff and fold into the chocolate mixture. Pour over the sponge finger biscuits. Put in the refrigerator and leave to chill for several hours.

Decorate with a little whipped cream and then sprinkle liberally with browned flaked almonds.

Serves 6

CHOCOLATE MOUSSE

A quick pudding to make, that is very popular with the young.

   1 packet 'dream topping'
   Milk
   2 oz (50 g) plain chocolate
   ½ oz (12½ g) gelatine
   3 tablespoons water
   14½-oz (411-g) can ready-to-serve custard
   1 chocolate Swiss roll
   A little whipped cream

Make the dream topping with the milk as instructed on the packet.

Break the chocolate into squares and put in a bowl and stand over a pan of simmering water until melted. Put the gelatine in a cup with the water and leave to soak for 3 minutes, then stand in the pan of simmering water and heat gently until dissolved; leave to cool slightly. Turn the custard into a bowl and beat lightly, add the melted chocolate and gelatine and stir in until evenly blended. Then fold in the dream topping.

Cut the Swiss roll into slices and arrange around the edge of a 2-pint (1-l) glass serving dish. Pour the mixture into the centre and leave in a cool place to set.

Decorate with swirls of cream.

Serves 4 – 6

LEMON CREAM CHEESE

This is a quick creamy pudding made in the electric blender. It is very rich so is best served in glasses or syllabub cups.

> 2 large lemons
> 2 oz (50 g) caster sugar
> ½ lb (225 g) curd or cream cheese
> ¼ pint (150 ml) double cream
> 4 fresh lemon slices and a few pistachio nuts

Squeeze out the juice from both lemons and put in an electric blender with the sugar and cheese and blend well. Pour in the double cream and blend until just mixed. Divide the mixture between four individual glasses or cups and chill for several hours.

It is best eaten the day that it is made and served decorated with a twisted slice of fresh lemon and sprinkling of pistachio nuts.

Serves 4

SYLLABUB

This is a rich simple ending; serve with small thin shortbread biscuits.

> ½ pint (300 ml) double cream
> Juice of 1 lemon
> 2 tablespoons brandy
> 3 oz (75 g) caster sugar

Whisk all the ingredients together, until light but not thick, a day before required. Turn into four small glasses or syllabub cups and leave in the refrigerator until required.

Each portion may be decorated with a twisted slice of fresh lemon. Serve with shortbread biscuits.

Serves 4

OLD ENGLISH TRIFLE

Trifle is something that has gone very much out of fashion these days; but I welcome it back. It is best made in a shallow glass dish. If time is short make thick bought custard with the top of the milk, then whisk well in an electric blender; the result will be beautifully creamy and the colour and texture lighter.

8-oz (227-g) can pears
6 individual sponge cakes, split in half
Strawberry jam
2 oz (50 g) ratafia biscuits
12 maraschino cherries, chopped
1 tablespoon maraschino syrup
5 tablespoons sherry
3 egg yolks
1 oz (25 g) caster sugar
1 heaped teaspoon cornflour
$\frac{1}{2}$ pint (300 ml) milk
$\frac{1}{4}$ pint (150 ml) whipping cream
$\frac{1}{2}$ oz (12$\frac{1}{2}$ g) almonds, blanched, split and lightly
    toasted

Drain the pears, reserving the juice, and then cut the fruit into small pieces. Sandwich the sponge cakes together with strawberry jam and put with the pears on the bottom of a shallow 2-pint (a good litre) serving dish. Top with the ratafia biscuits and sprinkle over the chopped cherries, pear juice, maraschino syrup and sherry.

Mix together the egg yolks, sugar and cornflour. Warm the milk in a saucepan over a low heat until it is hand-hot and pour it onto the yolk mixture, stirring constantly. Return the mixture to the saucepan and cook gently, stirring until it thickens; do not allow to boil or the custard will curdle. Allow to cool, then pour over the sponge cakes and leave to set before serving.

Lightly whisk the cream until it is thick and then spread it over the custard. Spike with the almonds and serve.

Serves 6

HOT APRICOT BRÛLÉE

It is best to make this in individual dishes. I also make it with apples and pears.

    15½-oz (439-g) can apricots, drained
    ½ pint (300 ml) double cream
    2 eggs
    ½ teaspoon vanilla essence
    4 level tablespoons demerara sugar

Heat the oven to 325°F, 160°C, gas no. 3.

Divide the apricots between four ¼-pint (150-ml) individual oven-proof dishes or six ramekins.

Beat the cream, eggs and vanilla essence together and pour over the apricots, dividing equally between the dishes. Bake in the oven for 25 minutes or until set. Then remove and sprinkle the tops thickly with demerara sugar and put under a hot grill for 2 to 3 minutes for the sugar to melt and go golden brown. Serve at once.

Serves 4 – 6

MELON AND RASPBERRY BRÛLÉE

This is another very quick dessert. You need individual flame-proof dishes of about ½ pint (300 ml) capacity or a large shallow flame-proof dish.

    1 honeydew melon
    8 oz (225 g) raspberries
    About 2 oz (50 g) icing sugar
    3 to 4 tablespoons white rum or brandy
    ½ pint (300 ml) double cream
    Light soft brown sugar

Cut the melon in quarters and remove all the seeds, then cut the flesh from the skin and cut into small dice. Place in a bowl with the raspberries and sprinkle with the icing sugar. Cover and chill thoroughly for several hours.

Divide the mixture between six individual oven-proof dishes or a large oven-proof dish, about 2½ pint (1.4 l) capacity. The size will vary with the size of the melon, but it is important to leave room for the cream to bubble up in the cooking.

Sprinkle the rum or brandy over the fruit. Lightly whip the cream until it just forms soft peaks and spread over the top of the fruit. Scatter the sugar quite thickly, but at random, over the top of the cream so that not all of the surface is covered.

Put under a hot grill until the sugar begins to darken and goes a deep golden brown.

Serves 6 – 8

CRÈME BRÛLÉE

This is sheer luxury, and is not difficult to make. Choose a shallow buttered dish that will withstand being put under the grill. This is a very good way of using up surplus egg yolks. Make the cream custard part a day ahead, then put the sugar topping on 3 hours before serving.

    4 egg yolks
    1 oz (25 g) caster sugar or vanilla sugar
    1 pint (600 ml) single cream
    About 2 oz (50 g) demerara sugar

Heat the oven to 325°F, 160°C, gas no. 3. Well butter a shallow oven-proof dish about 1½ pint (900 ml) size or six to eight small individual dishes.

Beat the egg yolks with the sugar or vanilla sugar; if you do not have vanilla sugar, add a little vanilla essence. Heat the cream to scalding (180°F) and gradually beat into the egg yolks.

Pour into the dish or divide between individual dishes, stand in a baking tin half filled with warm water and bake in the oven for 45 minutes or until set. If using small dishes they will only need about 25 to 30 minutes cooking time. Take out and leave to cool.

Sprinkle the top with demerara sugar to about ¼-inch (½-cm) thickness and put under a hot grill. Watch carefully until the sugar melts and then caramelizes to a golden brown.

Remove and chill before serving for about 3 hours. This gives time for the hard caramel topping to become slightly less hard and easy to crack and serve. If you leave it considerably longer the caramel will melt and soften which is not nearly so attractive and does not taste as good.

Serves 6 – 8

In praise of fresh fruit

So far we have had filling puddings, fattening puddings, light rich puddings and rich, rich puddings, ones that are easy to freeze and others which must not go near the freezer. Now we come to the cook's great stand-by – fresh fruit. Fruits with a short season, like strawberries and raspberries, need very little to boost them. Simply because their season is so short, most people are content to guzzle as much as they can while they can. But fresh fruit can be used in so many puddings and all of them round off a meal in the lightest, most refreshing way.

As far as freezing is concerned, most raw fruit dishes are better freshly made. Those, however, which use cooked fruit, such as Summer Pudding, or fruit in a syrup, lose none of their pleasant quality when frozen. Fruit fools freeze very successfully provided that you use equal quantities of fruit purée and whipped cream in the preparation. Beware of freezing dishes to which yogurt or custard have been added. These tend to become watery when thawed.

JUST BAKED APPLES

These are so simple that we often forget to make them. Bake them when you are making an oven-baked first course; they will look after themselves on the shelf below.

    4 large cooking apples
    2 oz (50 g) soft brown sugar
    2 oz (50 g) butter
    2 tablespoons water

Heat the oven to 350°F, 180°C, gas no. 4.

Wipe the apples and remove the cores, using a sharp knife or corer, and make a slit around the centre of each apple. Place the apples in an oven-proof dish and fill the centres with the sugar and place a knob of butter on top of each apple and pour around the water.

Bake in the oven for 40 to 45 minutes until the apples are puffy and soft. The water with the sugar and butter in the apples will make a sauce to serve spooned over the apples. Serve hot with thick cream or ice cream.

Serves 4

BANANA CREAM

A really simple creamy pudding. Serve in demi-tasse coffee cups, small glasses or ramekins.

   4 ripe bananas
   2 – 3 level tablespoons thin honey
   Juice of ½ a lemon
   ½ pint (300 ml) whipping cream
   Grated chocolate

Mash the bananas with the honey and lemon juice until fairly smooth.

Whisk the cream with an electric or hand rotary whisk until it forms soft peaks and then gently fold in the banana mixture with a spoon.

Turn into a 2-pint (1-l) glass serving dish. Chill for 2 hours and then serve sprinkled with plenty of grated chocolate.

Serves 4 – 6

APPLE AND ALMOND DESSERT CAKE

Some time ago I was doing a short cooking film which was being filmed in a hired kitchen and sitting on the middle shelf in the refrigerator was about three-quarters of this confection – looking so tempting. By the end of the day I just couldn't resist asking to taste it. I did, with cream, and it was mouth watering even cold. The recipe was warmly given to me, so here it is.

   5 oz (150 g) butter
   2 large eggs

   8 oz (225 g) caster sugar
   1 teaspoon almond essence
   8 oz (225 g) self-raising flour
   1½ teaspoons baking powder
   2 lb (900 g) cooking apples, before peeling (windfalls
     would do well)

Well grease a loose bottomed 10-inch (25-cm) round cake tin or spring form tin. If these are not available you could use a 9-inch (22.5-cm) square meat tin and line it with greased greaseproof paper, though even so you may find it difficult to get it out after baking.

Melt the butter in a pan over a medium heat; do not allow the butter to colour. Pour it into a roomy mixing bowl. Add the eggs, caster sugar and almond essence and beat well until mixed. Fold in the flour and baking powder and spread just under two-thirds of the mixture in the tin. Then straight away peel, core and slice the apples and arrange fairly evenly on top of the mixture in the tin. Spread the remaining mixture over the apples as evenly as you can. This is difficult as it sticks to the apple; it does not quite cover, but this does not matter.

Bake in the oven at 350°F, 180°C, gas no. 4 for about 1½ hours; the top will then be a pale golden brown and the apple tender when prodded with a skewer. Carefully push the cake out, having loosened the sides with a knife. Dust over very generously with icing sugar. Serve hot or warm as a pudding or cold as a dessert cake with lots of cream. To store keep covered with plastic wrap in the refrigerator.

Serves 12 large wedges

SUMMER PUDDING

Some of the best fruits to include in Summer Pudding are raspberries, strawberries, loganberries, blackberries or red currants. Don't let any one fruit overpower the pudding, and make sure that it is really wet and full of fruit. I never mind if the pudding collapses gently when it is turned out as it means that it is not too solid with bread! Make it in a fairly shallow dish so that when it is upturned it does not have a great weight to hold; a pudding basin often is too deep. A proportion of rhubarb and apple may be added to the stronger-flavoured fruits and helps to spin them out. Use fruits from the freezer if you have plenty in stock, mixing with fruits that are in season.

> 6 – 8 large, fairly thin, slices of white bread with the
>   crusts removed
> $\frac{1}{2}$ lb (225 g) rhubarb
> $\frac{1}{2}$ lb (225 g) black currants
> $\frac{1}{2}$ lb (225 g) granulated sugar
> 6 tablespoons water
> $\frac{1}{2}$ lb (225 g) small strawberries, or large ones halved
> $\frac{1}{2}$ lb (225 g) raspberries

Put one slice of bread on one side for the top; use the remainder to line the base and sides of a 2-pint (a good litre) round, fairly shallow, dish.

Put the rhubarb, cut into $\frac{1}{2}$-inch (1.25-cm) slices, with the black currants in a saucepan, add the sugar and water and bring to the boil and simmer for a few minutes until barely tender, stirring. Add the strawberries and raspberries and cook for a further minute.

Turn the mixture into the dish, place the slice of bread on the top and bend over the tops of the sliced bread at the sides towards the centre. Put a saucer on top, pressing down a little until the juice rises to the top of the dish.

Leave to soak until cold or overnight in the refrigerator. Turn out just before serving and serve with lots of cream.

Serves 4 – 6

SIMPLE FRESH FRUIT SALAD

I know that one should make a sugar syrup for fruit salad but as life gets busier I often take a short cut. First I peel and prepare the fruits that are likely to discolour and then I quickly prepare a citrus fruit and add it with caster sugar on top, maybe with some lemon juice – this helps keep the colour – and then, go on layering the fruit, finishing with caster sugar and citrus fruit. Cover and leave in the refrigerator overnight; in that time the sugar and the juice of the fruit make a syrup. For special occasions brandy or orange liqueur is sometimes added. Always serve the salad very cold. If you have sprigs of lemon balm, borage or mint use them to decorate.

FRUIT SALAD WITH A SUGAR SYRUP

4 oz (100 g) caster sugar
8 tablespoons water
Juice of $\frac{1}{2}$ a lemon
8 oz (225 g) large green grapes, peeled and pips
   removed
8 oz (225 g) eating apples, peeled, cored and sliced
2 oranges, peeled and segmented
1 small melon, peeled, seeded and cut into cubes
1 small pineapple, peeled, cored and cut into cubes
2 tablespoons orange liqueur

Dissolve the sugar in the water over a low heat. Cool, then stir in the lemon juice. Pour into a serving dish and stir in the fruit and liqueur. Chill thoroughly and serve with plenty of cream.

Serves 8

CHILLED GREEN FRUIT SALAD

Make this a day ahead and chill overnight. There is no need to make a syrup for this recipe, just sprinkle the sugar over the fruit as you prepare it.

2 Granny Smith apples, cored and sliced
2 pears, peeled, cored and sliced
Juice of 1 lemon
8 oz (225 g) caster sugar
8 oz (225 g) large green grapes
2 Kiwi fruits, sliced and peeled
1 small melon, peeled, seeded and cut into cubes

Place the apples and pears in a bowl and squeeze over the juice of the lemon to prevent discolouration. Sprinkle with some of the sugar and then cover with another layer of fruit and some more sugar. Continue until all the fruit has been added, finishing with a layer of sugar. Cover the bowl with a plate or piece of cling film and leave overnight in the refrigerator.

Turn into a glass serving dish, mixing lightly so that all the fruits are blended evenly. Serve with plenty of cream.

Serves 8

RHUBARB FOOL

This is an inexpensive and good way with rhubarb if you have a free supply in the garden. Serve on the day that it is made.

   1 lb (450 g) young rhubarb
   2 tablespoons water
   3 – 4 oz (75 g – 100 g) caster sugar
   17-fluid oz (510-ml) family brick vanilla ice cream
   A little pink colouring

Place the rhubarb, cut in short lengths, in a saucepan with the water. Cover and cook very gently until tender, this will take about 15 to 20 minutes. Remove from the heat and sieve into a bowl. Add sugar to taste and leave to become quite cold.

Remove the ice cream from the freezer and leave to soften at room temperature for about 10 minutes. Stir the ice cream into the purée and mix until well blended; if liked add a little pink colouring.

Turn into glass dish and serve with shortbread biscuits or brandy snaps.

Serves 4

BANANAS IN CHOCOLATE

One of the very first things I remember seeing my mother preparing in the kitchen for special friends were these bananas. They are inclined to stick to a wire tray so I do them on silicone paper and chill them well before serving. I remember hoping that some would not be quite perfect so I could try them too. These are very rich and some people will find that one makes a very adequate portion.

>   8 small bananas
>   8 oz (225 g) plain chocolate
>   A few chopped pistachio nuts or flaked browned
>   almonds

Peel the bananas and lay on a sheet of silicone paper or on a wire rack over a plate.

Break the chocolate into small pieces and melt slowly in a double saucepan or in a bowl over a pan of simmering water. Then carefully spoon over the bananas to coat completely, any chocolate that falls onto the paper or plate may be scraped up and used again when remelted.

Sprinkle the nuts on the top of the bananas whilst the chocolate is still warm.

Leave undisturbed for half an hour and then lift carefully onto a serving dish and chill thoroughly. Serve with Brandy Cream (see p. 45).

Serves 4 – 8

PINEAPPLE IN KIRSCH

This is such a simple idea that it is often forgotten. The Kirsch is not a must, just nice to make it extra special. Serve very cold.

1 pineapple
2 tablespoons caster sugar
2 tablespoons Kirsch

Slice off the leaf and stem end of the pineapple and keep the leaves on one side. Cut the pineapple across into ½-inch (1.25-cm) slices and, using a small sharp knife, cut off the skin from each slice.

Remove the tough centre core with a small pastry cutter or an apple corer. Arrange the slices on a flat serving dish and sprinkle with the sugar and Kirsch and leave in a cool place for at least 8 hours to chill thoroughly. When ready to serve, arrange the leaves so that they are standing upright in the centre of the dish and serve with thick whipped cream.

Serves 6

STRAWBERRIES WITH ORANGES

A lovely refreshing pudding that is very easy to make.

3 large oranges
1½ lb (675 g) fresh strawberries
3 oz (75 g) caster or icing sugar
Raspberry sauce (see Peach Melba, p. 150)

Peel the oranges, removing all the white pith. Divide the

oranges into segments, removing the membrane between each segment.

Hull the strawberries and if very large cut in half, otherwise leave whole. Mix them with the orange segments, place in a glass serving dish and sprinkle over the sugar. Leave in the refrigerator or a cool place for at least 4 hours or until the sugar has completely dissolved and the fruit is very well chilled.

Serve with a spoonful of raspberry sauce and plenty of lightly whipped cream.

Serves 6 – 8

CARAMELIZED ORANGES

These are whole oranges, peeled carefully, removing all the skin and pith, and then sliced and secured with a cocktail stick. They look great on a buffet table in a glass dish.

    6 oranges
    4 oz (100 g) granulated sugar
    5 tablespoons water
    2 tablespoons brandy or orange liqueur

Thinly peel the rind from two of the oranges with a potato peeler and cut into very fine julienne strips. Place these in a small saucepan, cover with cold water, bring to the boil and simmer for about 20 minutes or until tender. Drain and reserve on one side.

Slice both ends from the oranges, then, standing the fruit upright on a plate, slice down and around the oranges to remove all the peel and pith. Slice each orange across, removing any pips, and then reassemble into the original shape and secure with a cocktail stick. Place in a dish. Reserve all the orange juice on the plate and put it into a measure with the brandy or liqueur and make up to ¼ pint (150 ml) with water.

Place the sugar and 5 tablespoons of water in a small thick saucepan and stir over a low heat until the sugar has dissolved, then bring to the boil and cook rapidly to a rich dark caramel. Remove from the heat and stir in the orange juice mixture; be careful as it will splutter. Return the pan to the heat and warm until the caramel and orange juice have amalgamated to form a sauce. Pour over the oranges, leave to cool and then chill thoroughly overnight.

Next day transfer to a glass serving dish and pour over the syrup, sprinkle with the strips of orange rind and serve with lightly whipped cream.

Serves 6

PEARS IN RED WINE

Pears cooked in red wine make an attractive sweet and are very good when served for a dinner party.

      6 oz (175 g) granulated sugar
      ¼ pint (150 ml) water
      ¼ pint (150 ml) red wine
      Strip of lemon rind
      Small piece of cinnamon stick
      6 ripe dessert pears
      1 rounded teaspoon arrowroot
      1 oz (25 g) flaked browned almonds

Put the sugar, water, wine, lemon rind and cinnamon stick

in a pan and heat gently until the sugar has dissolved, stirring occasionally. Bring to the boil and simmer for a minute.

Keeping the stalks on the pears, remove all the peel and the eyes from the base of each pear. Put them in the syrup, cover and poach gently for 25 to 30 minutes until the pears are tender.

Carefully lift out the pears with a slotted spoon and arrange in a glass serving dish. Strain the syrup, which will measure a good ½ pint (300 ml). Blend the arrowroot with a little cold water in the empty saucepan and stir in the syrup. Return to the heat and bring to the boil, stirring until thickened. Cook for 2 minutes, then spoon over the pears and leave to cool. When quite cold cover and chill thoroughly for several hours.

Sprinkle with the almonds and serve with a bowl of thick cream.

Serves 6

On the continental kick and special gâteaux

As I have said before, most European nations are not a patch on the British when it comes to puddings. Nevertheless, there are a few Continental specialities which have found a warm place in British hearts, and these are included here.

MILLE FEUILLES

I use bought puff pastry for these and home-made confectioner's custard. Cut en-block with a sawing action into slices after icing. They are very messy to eat and are best tackled with a fork.

8 oz (227 g) packet puff pastry, just thawed
Confectioner's custard:
2 eggs
2 oz (50 g) vanilla sugar
1 oz (25 g) plain flour
½ pint (300 ml) milk
A little vanilla essence
Raspberry jam
About 2 oz – 5 oz (50 g – 150 g) icing, sugar, sieved
Lemon juice

Heat the oven to 450°F, 230°C, gas no. 8.

Roll out the pastry thinly to a rectangle 11 inches × 9 inches (28 cm × 22.5 cm). Prick well and lift onto a baking tray and bake in the oven for 15 to 20 minutes until well risen and golden brown. Cool on a wire rack and then cut in half lengthwise.

Now make the custard: beat the eggs and sugar together with the flour and a little of the milk. Heat the remaining milk almost to boiling point and pour onto the egg mixture, stirring continuously. Return to the pan, stir over a low heat until it boils, stirring all the time until the mixture has thickened. Add a little vanilla essence to taste. Remove from the heat and leave to cool, stirring from time to time.

Spread the top of one piece of pastry with the jam and cover with the pastry cream and then top with the other piece of pastry and lightly press together. Blend the icing sugar in a small bowl with just enough lemon juice to give a coating consistency. Coat the top of the mille feuille and leave to set. Then cut into six slices and arrange on a serving plate.

Serves 6

FRENCH PROFITEROLES

These look spectacular for a party. Fill them with cream and pour the sauce over, ideally just before serving.

2 oz (50 g) butter
$\frac{1}{4}$ pint (150 ml) water
$2\frac{1}{2}$ oz ($62\frac{1}{2}$ g) plain flour
2 eggs, beaten

Filling:
$\frac{1}{2}$ pint (300 ml) double cream

Icing:
$1\frac{1}{2}$ oz (40 g) butter
1 oz (25 g) cocoa
4 oz (100 g) icing sugar
3 – 4 tablespoons evaporated milk

Heat the oven to 425°F, 220°C, gas no. 7 and grease a baking tray.

Put the butter and water in a small pan and bring to boil slowly to allow the butter to melt. Remove from the heat and add the flour all at once and beat until it forms a ball. Gradually beat in the eggs a little at a time to make a smooth shiny paste.

Put the mixture into a piping bag fitted with a ½-inch (1.25-cm) plain nozzle and pipe into 20 blobs on the baking tray and bake for 10 minutes. Then reduce the heat to 375°F, 190°C, gas no. 5 for a further 15 to 20 minutes until well risen and golden brown. Split one side of each bun to allow the steam to escape and leave to cool on a wire rack. Fill each bun with whipped cream.

Now make the icing: melt the butter in a small pan and stir in the cocoa and cook gently for a minute. Remove the pan from the heat and stir in the sieved icing sugar and evaporated milk, beat well until starting to thicken. Then spear each bun with a fork and dip into the icing, to just cover the tops. Pile up in a pyramid as each one is finished. Serve the same day.

Serves 6 – 8

LEMON GRIESTORTE

Keep in the refrigerator until just before serving, then dust the top with plenty of icing sugar.

    3 eggs, separated
    4 oz (100 g) caster sugar
    ½ teaspoon almond essence
    2 oz (50 g) ground semolina
    ½ oz (12½g) ground almonds

Filling:
 ¼ pint (150 ml) whipping cream
 4 level tablespoons home-made lemon curd
 Icing sugar

Heat the oven to 350°F, 180°C, gas no. 4. Line an 8-inch (20-cm) cake tin with greased greaseproof paper and dust with flour.

Put the egg yolks and caster sugar in a heat-proof bowl over a pan of hot water and whisk until the mixture is pale and thick. Remove from the heat and fold in the almond essence, semolina and ground almonds. Whisk the egg whites until they form soft peaks, then fold into the mixture.

Turn into the cake tin and bake in the oven for 30 minutes or until the cake is well risen and pale golden. Turn out and leave the cake to cool on a wire rack.

Split the cake in half. Whisk the cream until starting to thicken and then whisk in the lemon curd until thick and the cream will hold a soft peak. Sandwich the cake together, keep in the refrigerator until required, then dust the top with plenty of icing sugar and serve.

Serves 6

STRAWBERRY AND CREAM DESSERT CAKE

This is simply a good fatless sponge. Either whisk eggs and sugar over a pan of hot water if using a hand whisk or, if you have an electric mixer, just whisk in in the bowl, without a pan of hot water, until the mixture is light and creamy. When cold fill with the strawberry and cream filling. Far nicer, I think, than Strawberry Shortcake, it also makes the first strawberries go a long way.

    4 eggs, at room temperature
    4 oz (100 g) caster sugar, warmed
    4 oz (100 g) self-raising flour
    ¼ pint (150 ml) whipping cream
    ½ lb (225 g) strawberries
    2 – 3 tablespoons cointreau
    A little caster sugar to taste
    Icing sugar

Grease and line with greased greaseproof paper two 8-inch (20-cm) sandwich cake tins. Heat the oven to 375°F, 190°C, gas no. 5.

Put the eggs and sugar in a heat-proof bowl placed over a pan of hot water and whisk until the mixture is thick, white and creamy and the whisk leaves a trail when lifted out. Remove from the heat and whisk for a further 2 minutes. Sift in the flour and carefully fold in.

Divide the mixture between the two tins and bake for 20 minutes or until the sponge is a pale golden brown and springs back when lightly pressed with a finger tip. Turn out and leave to cool on a wire rack.

Whisk the cream until it forms soft peaks. Hull the strawberries and cut them in quarters. Fold them into the cream with the cointreau and a little caster sugar to taste. Fill the sponges with this mixture. Place on a serving dish and chill for 3 hours. When ready to serve dust the top with plenty of icing sugar.

Serves 8

DANISH LAYER CAKE

This takes time to make but is well worth the effort. The cake is composed of very thin Cinnamon Shortbreads layered together with cream and raspberry jam.

6½ oz (187½ g) butter
6½ oz (187½ g) caster sugar
8½ oz (237½ g) flour
2 level teaspoons ground cinnamon
½ pint (300 ml) double cream
3 tablespoons top of the milk
Raspberry jam
Icing sugar
8 walnut halves

Heat the oven to 400°F, 200°C, gas no. 6 and thoroughly grease plenty of baking sheets.

Cream the butter until it is soft, then add the sugar and continue to beat until the mixture is pale and fluffy. Sift the flour and cinnamon together and add to the butter mixture a tablespoonful at a time. The last few spoonfuls may have to be worked in by hand. Knead lightly and then divide the mixture into eight equal pieces.

Put one piece of dough onto the baking tray and press out very thinly with the fingers to form a 7-inch (17.5-cm) circle. It is a good idea to do this inside a plain flan ring as it gives a nice even circle. Bake in the oven for about 8 minutes until a pale golden brown. Remove from the oven and leave to cool for a few minutes before transferring to a wire rack. Repeat with the other seven pieces of dough, baking two or three at a time, depending on the number of trays that you have.

Whisk the cream and milk together until they will form a soft peak and use this to sandwich the layers together with the jam, leaving a little cream over for decoration. Leave to stand for 3 to 4 hours before serving to allow the mixture to soften slightly.

Place on a serving dish and sprinkle the top with icing sugar, pipe eight swirls of cream evenly around the edge and place a walnut half on top.

Serves 8

Easy ice creams and sorbets

For many people, ices and sorbets are the best kind of pudding of all. Children, especially, seem to love them, whatever the weather. Even when there is ten degrees of frost outside and a request to take the dog for a walk is met with cries of anguish, they will still fall on a dish of ice cream with every sign of relish.

Home-made ice cream is a rare luxury in these days of freezer centres and commercial family packs. Using my very creamy basic recipe it is very easy to make and provides an opportunity to try out less usual ingredients, such as gooseberries.

It goes without saying, of course, that all the dishes described here freeze well. To get the 'soft scoop' feel thaw slightly in the refrigerator before serving, but remember to put the ice cream back in the freezer afterwards! For a special occasion, pile scoopfuls of ice cream or sorbet in a bowl, cover with clear cling film and return to the freezer. Just before taking to the table, remove the film and decorate the pile with fresh mint, strawberries or some other suitable garnish. Having the ice cream already separated into scoopfuls makes serving much easier and the dish itself will look more attractive.

THE BASIC SPECIAL ICE CREAM

I find this the perfect ice cream to make. It is rich and creamy. I rarely make any other but just add variations to this. I would not tackle the French custard-based ice cream as water crystals always appear however often you re-whisk during freezing. This special ice cream needs no whisking during freezing, it goes into the freezer thick and creamy and just needs to be frozen and solidified. My favourite flavours are lemon, coffee, rum and raisin and black currant.

  4 eggs, separated
  4 oz (100 g) caster sugar
  ½ pint (300 ml) whipping cream

Whisk the yolks in a small bowl until blended. In a larger bowl whisk the egg whites with a hand rotary or electric whisk on high speed until they are stiff, then whisk in the sugar a teaspoonful at a time; the whites will get stiffer and stiffer as the sugar is added.

Whisk the cream until it forms soft peaks and then fold it into the meringue mixture with the egg yolks. Add vanilla essence if liked.

Turn the mixture into a 2½-pint (1.4-l) container, cover, label and freeze.

Leave to thaw at room temperature for 5 minutes then serve in scoops in small glasses or dishes.

Serves 6 – 8

AMERICAN MINT

Add half a bar of crushed seaside rock to the ice cream before freezing. It gives a lovely crunchy taste with pink specks.

FRESH MINT

Add a handful of finely chopped mint (chopped with a little caster sugar) to the ice cream before freezing.

ORANGE CHOCOLATE CHIP

Add about 2 oz (50 g) broken chocolate orange sticks to the ice cream before freezing.

TOFFEE BUTTERSCOTCH

Add about 4 oz (100 g) crushed butterscotch to the ice cream before freezing.

RASPBERRY, STRAWBERRY OR GOOSEBERRY

Use double cream and stir in ¼ pint (150 ml) fruit purée to the ice cream just before freezing and add a little colouring if necessary.

PINEAPPLE

Use double cream. Cut the flesh from a small pineapple, add the juice of a small lemon and 2 oz (50 g) icing sugar and purée in a blender. Then freeze until just set and fold it into the ice cream just before freezing.

TUTTI FRUITI

Add about 4 oz (100 g) chopped glacé pineapple, raisins, dried apricots, cherries and angelica soaked overnight in 4 tablespoons brandy to plump them up. Fold into the ice cream just before freezing.

COFFEE, RUM AND RAISIN

Add 2 tablespoons coffee essence and 3 tablespoons rum to about 4 oz (100 g) chopped, stoned raisins and soak overnight. Fold in just before freezing.

BLACK CURRANT

Use double cream and add about 6 tablespoons undiluted blackcurrant drink (Ribena) to the cream and fold into the meringue mixture.

LEMON

Use double cream and the grated rind and juice of 2 lemons. Whisk the cream with the lemon rind and juice until it forms soft peaks, then fold into the meringue as usual.

PROPER PEACH MELBA

There is nothing like the real thing – decidedly for grown-ups! Children, I find, are totally happy with a posh tall glass, bought dairy ice cream, canned peaches and raspberry sauce; it is the presentation that they love.

    4 fresh peaches
    ½ lb (225 g) caster sugar
    1 pint (600 ml) water

Sauce:
    ½ lb (225 g) fresh raspberries
    4 oz (100 g) icing sugar
    Vanilla ice cream (see p. 147)
    ¼ pint (150 ml) double cream, whipped

Peel, halve and stone the peaches. Put the caster sugar and

water in a large shallow pan and simmer together, stirring occasionally until the sugar has dissolved. Put the peaches in a single layer in the pan and simmer gently for about 10 to 12 minutes, then remove from the heat and leave to cool in the syrup. When quite cold, lift out the peaches with a slotted spoon.

For the sauce: place the raspberries in an electric blender for a few seconds with the icing sugar until smooth and then sieve into a bowl to remove all the pips.

Place a portion of ice cream in the base of four sundae glasses and arrange two peach halves on top of each portion. Pour over some raspberry sauce and pipe a swirl of cream on each sundae. Serve at once.

Serves 4

PRALINE ICE CREAM

This is such a good ice cream. It is quite unexpected to come across crunchy pieces of caramel.

$1\frac{1}{2}$ oz (40 g) whole unblanched almonds
$5\frac{1}{2}$ oz ($162\frac{1}{2}$ g) caster sugar
4 eggs
$\frac{1}{2}$ pint (300 ml) whipping cream

Put the almonds with $1\frac{1}{2}$ oz (40 g) caster sugar in a heavy pan and place over a low heat, stirring occasionally until the sugar has melted and is beginning to caramelize; this will take about 15 minutes. Continue to cook until the mixture is an even golden brown and nuts are glazed. Remove from the heat and pour onto an oiled enamel plate or a baking tray. Leave until quite firm and cold then turn into a grinder and grind coarsely.

Separate the eggs, place the yolks in a small bowl and whisk until well blended. In an other larger bowl, whisk the egg whites until stiff and then whisk in the remaining sugar a teaspoonful at a time. Whisk the cream until it forms soft peaks and fold into the meringue mixture with the egg yolks and praline.

Turn into a 2½-pint (1.4-l) rigid container, cover, label and freeze.

Remove from the refrigerator and leave to stand for 5 minutes, then serve in scoops in individual glasses with a brandy snap.

Serves 6 – 8

STRAWBERRY ICE CREAM

Evaporated milk is a good substitute for cream as long as you have a strong flavour such as strawberries; it adds richness and lightness and the lemon takes away the evaporated milk taste.

  2 level teaspoons powdered gelatine
  3 tablespoons water
  1 lb (450 g) strawberries
  1 large 14½-oz (410-g) can evaporated milk, chilled
      overnight.
  6 oz (175 g) caster sugar
  Juice of ½ a large lemon

Place the gelatine in a small bowl or cup with the cold water and leave to stand for 3 minutes until it becomes a sponge. Stand the bowl in a pan of simmering water and leave to dissolve until the gelatine has become quite clear.

Purée the strawberries in a blender and stir in the gelatine. Whisk the evaported milk with an electric or hand rotary whisk until thick enough to hold a trail left by the whisk; then whisk in the sugar, strawberry purée and lemon juice.

Turn into a 3½-pint (2-l) rigid container, cover, label and freeze. When required leave to stand at room temperature for 10 to 15 minutes, then serve in scoops in glasses and decorate with a whole strawberry and a fancy wafer biscuit.

Serves 8 – 10

BROWN BREAD ICE CREAM

This sounds most uninteresting but it is truly delicious; there are caramelized crunchy pieces in a lovely creamy ice cream.

  1½ oz (40 g) fresh brown breadcrumbs
  1½ oz (40 g) soft brown sugar
  2 eggs, separated
  1 oz (25 g) caster sugar
  ¼ pint (150 ml) double cream

Place the breadcrumbs on an enamel or foil plate with the soft brown sugar and toast under a hot grill until golden brown and caramelized, stirring occasionally. Keep a sharp eye whilst the crumbs are browning, and wait for them to turn a dark horse-chestnut colour. This will take 5 to 8 minutes. Leave to become quite cold.

Whisk the egg yolks in a small bowl until well blended. In another bowl whisk the egg white with a hand rotary whisk or an electric whisk until stiff, then whisk in the caster sugar a teaspoonful at a time. Whisk the cream until it forms soft peaks, then fold into the egg whites with the yolks and breadcrumbs. Turn into a 1½-pint (900-ml) container, cover, label and freeze.

Leave to thaw at room temperature for 5 minutes then serve in scoops in glass dishes.

Serves 4

MELON CREAM ICE

A delicious ice cream for a special occasion; make it when melons are at their cheapest and best.

Half an Ogen or Galia melon
Juice of 2 lemons
3 sprigs of young mint
4 eggs, separated
4 oz (100 g) caster sugar
½ pint (300 ml) double cream

Remove the seeds from the melon and scoop out the flesh from the shell and purée in a blender with the lemon juice and mint leaves until smooth. Turn into a rigid container and freeze until mushy.

Whisk the yolks in a small bowl until blended. In another bowl whisk the egg whites with a hand rotary whisk or an electric whisk on high speed until they are stiff, then whisk in the sugar a teaspoonful at a time. Whisk the cream until it forms soft peaks, then fold into the egg-white mixture together with the yolks and partially frozen melon purée.

Turn into a 2½-pint (1.5-l) rigid container, cover label and freeze.

Leave to thaw at room temperature for 5 minutes, then serve in scoops in glass dishes. Garnish each dish with a small sprig of fresh mint.

Serves 6 – 8

FAMILY CHOCOLATE ICE CREAM

Using evaporated milk makes this an inexpensive rich ice cream. Cocoa gives a strong chocolate flavour. Chilling the can of evaporated milk means that you get more volume and that it is easy to whisk.

    1 oz (25 g) cocoa
    4 tablespoons boiling water
    4 eggs, separated
    5 oz (150 g) caster sugar
    $14\frac{1}{2}$-oz (410-g) can evaporated milk, chilled overnight

Put the cocoa in a small bowl with the water and stir until well blended and smooth. Leave it to cool and then beat in the egg yolks. Whisk the egg whites with an electric or rotary hand whisk on high speed until they are stiff, then whisk in the sugar a spoonful at a time.

Whisk the evaporated milk until it just holds a soft peak, then fold it into the egg whites together with the chocolate mixture. Turn into a $3\frac{1}{2}$-pint (2-l) rigid container. Cover, label and freeze, then use as required.

Leave to thaw at room temperature for 5 minutes, then serve in scoops in individual dishes or glasses with a wafer or crisp biscuit.

Serves 8

LEMON SORBET

The most refreshing of all the sorbets.

    6 lemons
    ½ pint (300 ml) water
    6 oz (175 g) sugar
    1 egg white

Peel the rind thinly from the bottom of each lemon, using a potato peeler. Put these pieces of rind in a saucepan with the water and sugar and heat gently until the sugar has dissolved, then simmer for 10 minutes. Remove from the heat and leave to cool.

Cut the tops off the lemons and scoop out all the flesh, using a grapefruit knife or pointed spoon. Put the flesh into a bowl with any juice, reserve the shells and tops.

Remove any pips from the flesh, then purée it in a blender and strain. Strain the sugar syrup onto the lemon purée and mix well. Turn into a rigid container, cover and freeze until half frozen.

Trim a little from the bottom of the lemon shells so that they will stand upright. Put the lemon shells and lids into the freezer to chill. Whisk the egg white until stiff. Turn the half-frozen lemon mixture into a bowl and whisk until smooth. Fold in the egg white and then pile the mixture into the lemon shells and put on the lids. Wrap individually in foil, label and freeze.

When required to serve, unwrap and leave to thaw in the refrigerator for about 30 minutes before serving.

Serves 6

ORANGE SORBET

A delicious sorbet that is so easy to make.

6 oz (175 g) sugar
¾ pint (450 ml) water
6½ oz (185 g) can frozen orange juice, thawed
2 egg whites

Dissolve the sugar in the water and bring to the boil, then simmer uncovered for 10 minutes. Turn the frozen orange juice into a bowl and pour on the sugar syrup. Leave to cool and then pour into a 1-pint (600-ml) ice cube tray and freeze to a mushy consistency.

Whisk the egg whites until thick and foamy but not dry. Fold into the orange mixture and return to the freezer until firm; cover and label. When required leave the sorbet to soften slightly in the refrigerator for 5 minutes then serve spooned into glasses.

Serves 4

RASPBERRY SORBET

A sorbet with a rich and glorious colour to it. You may be wondering why it is necessary to both purée and sieve the raspberries; the blender speeds up the process by liquifying the raspberries first, then it is only necessary to sieve so that all the pips are removed.

    1 lb (450 g) raspberries
    6 oz (175 g) sugar
    ½ pint (300 ml) water
    Juice of 1 orange
    3 egg whites

Purée the raspberries in a blender then pass through a nylon sieve and discard all the pips.

Put the sugar and water in a pan and heat gently until the sugar has dissolved, then bring to the boil and simmer for 5 minutes. Remove from the heat and stir in the raspberry purée and orange juice. Pour into a bowl and leave to cool.

Put into a 3½-pint (2-l) polythene container and place in the freezer and leave until partially frozen.

Whisk the egg whites with an electric or hand rotary whisk until stiff and then whisk in the partially frozen purée a tablespoonful at a time. Return to the container, cover, label and freeze.

Serve in scoops in glasses with a crisp wafter biscuit. They look lovely if decorated with a whole fresh raspberry and a small sprig of mint.

Serves 8

Index

Almond and apple dessert cake 124–5
Almond and apricot pancakes 51
Almond and black cherry cheese-cake (cooked) 77–8
Almond and mincemeat pie 21–2
American mint ice cream 148
Ann's cinnamon and apple pancakes 51
Apple and almond dessert cake 124–5
Apple and apricot steamed pudding 31
Apple and blackberry pudding 29
Apple with brown sugar crumble 39–40
Apple Charlotte 38–9
Apple and cinnamon pancakes 51
Apple dumplings, baked 44
Apple flan, French 15–16
Apple kuchen 54
Apple pie 9–10
Apples, just baked 123
Apricot and almond pancakes 51
Apricot and lemon mousse 66–7
Apricot and lemon pudding 37
Apricot brûlée, hot 116–17
Apricot tart, open 20–1

Apricot yogurt fool 101
Apricots, dried, to freeze 3

Baked apple dumplings 44
Baked apples 123
Baked custard 98
Baked jam roly poly 33
Baked macaroni milk pudding 100
Baked rice milk pudding 99–100
Baked tapioca milk pudding 100
Bakewell tart 12–13
Banana cream 124
Bananas in chocolate 130
Batter pudding (apple kuchen) 54
Batter, uncooked, to store 47
Black cherry and almond cheese-cake, cooked 77–8
Blackcurrant ice cream 150
Blackcurrant upside down pudding 37–8
Blackcurrants, freezing 3
Blackberry and apple pudding 29
Blackberry mousse, fresh 64–5
'Blind baking' 7–8
Bramble and apple pancakes 52
Brandy butter 45
Brandy and chocolate layer 109–10

Brandy cream 45
Bread and butter pudding 41–2
Bread pudding, Mary Norwak's
    42–3
Brown bread ice cream 153–4
Brown meringues 84
Brown sugar and apple crumble
    39–40
Butterscotch ice cream 148
Buying 2–3, 4–5
  for freezing 2–3
  ingredients 2–3, 4–5
  quantities 2–3
  for storing 2–3

Cake or pudding 42–3, 124–5
  Apple and almond dessert cake
    124–5
  Mary Norwak's bread pudding
    42–3
Caramel custard, to keep 95
Caramelized oranges 132–3
Cheesecake, to freeze 73
  to refrigerate 73
Cheesecake, cooked, black cherry
    and almond 77–8
Cheesecakes, uncooked 75–9
  Ginger and rhubarb 78–9
  Grapefruit 76–7
  Orange 75–6
  Rhubarb and ginger 78–9
Children's fare 47, 49, 81, 95, 113,
    145
Chilled sharp lemon soufflé 61–2
Chocolate, bananas in 130
Chocolate beacon 107–8
Chocolate and brandy layer 109–
    110
Chocolate ice cream, family 155
Chocolate meringue gâteau 87–8
Chocolate mousse 113
Chocolate mousse, rich 67–8

Chocolate pudding 34–5
Chocolate roulade 108–9
Chocolate soufflé, hot 59–60
Chocolate whisky gunge 112
Christmas plum pudding 32
Cinnamon and apple pancakes
    51
Classic pancakes 50
Coffee, rum and raisin ice cream
    149
Coffee soufflé, hot 61
Coffee walnut layer 111–12
Containers, storage 3–4
  soufflé 59
Continental specialities 137–43
  Danish layer cake 142–3
  French profiteroles 138–9
  Lemon griestorte 139–40
  Mille feuilles 137–8
  Profiteroles, French 138–9
  Strawberry and cream dessert
    cake 140–1
Cream puddings 105–19
  Apricot brûlée, hot 116–17
  Banana cream 124
  Brandy and chocolate layer
    109–10
  Chocolate beacon 107–8
  Chocolate and brandy layer
    109–10
  Chocolate roulade 108–9
  Crème brûlée 118–19
  Lemon cream cheese 114
  Lemon cream tart 18
  Melon and raspberry brûlée
    117–18
  Raspberry and melon brûlée
    117–18
  Syllabub 114–15
  Walnut coffee layer 111–12
Cream, to store 3
  thick, real pouring 46

Crème brûlée 118–19
Crème caramel 102–3
Crêpes Suzette 53–4
Crisp fruit fritters 55
Custard skin, to prevent 97
Custard tart, English 22–3
Custards 97–8
  Baked custard 98
  pouring custard 97
  trifle custard 98

Danish layer cake 142–3
Defrosting 4
Double crust pie 7

English custard tart 22–3
English trifle, old 115–16
Essences 4–5
  bought 4
  home-made 4–5
Eve's pudding 35–6

Flan, defined 7
  French apple 15–16
Flavours 4–5
  bought 4
  home-made 4–5
Foil containers 3–4
Fool, to freeze 121
Fools 101, 121, 129–30
  Apricot yogurt 101
  fruit 121
  Rhubarb 129–30
Freezer 2–5
Freezing 2–3, 3, 4, 8, 25, 47, 49–50,
  57, 73, 81, 105, 121, 145
  apricots, dried 3
  black currants 3
  cheesecakes 73
  'don'ts' 4, 105, 121
  fools 121
  fruit 3, 121

ice cream 145
ingredients 2–3
pancakes 47, 49–50
pastry 8
Pavlovas 81
soufflés, cold 57
times 4
winter puddings 25
French apple flan 15–16
French pancakes 56
French profiteroles 138–9
Fritters, crisp fruit 55
Fruit fools 121
Fruit, freezing 3, 121
Fruit meringues 81
Fruit Pavlova 91–2
Fruit pie, Midsummer 10–11
Fruit, fresh, in puddings 121–34
  Almond and apple dessert cake
    124–5
  Apples, just baked 123
  Banana cream 124
  Bananas in chocolate 130
  Caramelized oranges 132–3
  Fruit fritters 55
  Fruit salad, green, chilled 128–9
  meringues 81
  Fruit pie 10–11
  Fruit salad, simple, fresh 127
  Fruit salad with sugar syrup 128
  Green fruit salad, chilled 128–9
  Oranges, caramelized 132–3
  Pears in red wine 133–4
  Pineapple in Kirsch 131
  Rhubarb fool 129–30
  Strawberries with oranges 131–
    132
  Summer pudding 126–7
Fun pudding 92–3

Gâteaux 87–8, 135–43
  Chocolate meringue 87–8

Gâteaux – *continued*
  Ginger and pineapple meringue layer 86
  Ginger and rhubarb cheesecake (cold, cooked) 78–9
  Gooseberry ice cream 149
  Gooseberry shortcake 19
  Grapefruit cheesecake, cold 76–7
  Green fruit salad, chilled 128–9

Hazelnut meringue with chestnuts 88–9

Ice cream, basic special 147–8
  to decorate 145
  to freeze 145
  to refrigerate 145
  to serve 145
Ice creams 145–55
  American mint 148
  Black currant 150
  Brown bread 153–4
  Chocolate, family 155
  Coffee, rum and raisin 149
  Gooseberry 149
  Lemon 150
  Melon cream 154–5
  Mint, fresh 148
  Orange chocolate chip 148
  Peach Melba 150–1
  Pineapple 149
  Praline 151–2
  Raspberry 149
  Strawberry 149, 152–3
  Toffee butterscotch 148
  Tutti frutti 149

Jam roly poly, baked 33
Jane Grigson's Sussex Pond pudding 28–9
Junket 99

Larder 5–6
Lemon and apricot mousse 66–7
Lemon and apricot pudding 37
Lemon cream cheese 114
Lemon cream tart 18
Lemon griestorte 139–40
Lemon ice cream 150
Lemon meringue pie 16–18
Lemon sorbet 156
Lemon soufflé, chilled 61–2
Lemon soufflé, hot 60
Lemon soufflé omelette 70
Lemon soufflé pudding, hot 70–1
Lemon sugar 5
Lime mousse, fresh 68–9

Macaroni pudding, baked 100
Margaret's Pavlova 90–1
Mary Norwak's bread pudding 42–3
Melon cream ice 154–5
Melon and raspberry brûlée 117–18
Meringue puddings 16–18, 81, 84–9, 92–4
  Celebration fruit meringue 84–5
  Chocolate meringue gâteau 87–8
  Fun pudding 92–3
  Ginger and pineapple meringue layer 86
  Hazelnut with chestnuts 88–9
  Lemon meringue pie 16–18
  Meringue layers 85–6
  Pineapple and ginger meringue layer 86
  Pineapple meringue pudding 93–4
  Swiss hazelnut meringue with chestnuts 88–9
Meringues 81–9, 92–4
  brown 84
  celebration fruit 84–5

double 83–4
  fillings 81
  fruit 81
  layers 85–6
  storing 81
  teatime 81
Midnight mousse 65–6
Midsummer fruit pie 10–11
Milk pudding, refrigerating 95
Milk puddings 95–104
  Baked custard 98
  Baked macaroni 100
  Baked rice 99–100
  Baked tapioca 100
  Norwegian cream 103–4
Mille feuilles 137–8
Mincemeat and almond pie 21–2
Mincemeat tart 11–12
Mint ice cream, American 148
Mint ice cream, fresh 148
Mousses 62–8
  Apricot and lemon 66–7
  Blackberry 64–5
  Chocolate 113
  Chocolate, rich 67–8
  Fresh blackberry 64–5
  Fresh lime 68–9
  Lemon and apricot 66–7
  Midnight 65–6
  Pineapple 62–3
  Pineapple cheesecake 63–4
  Rich chocolate 67–8

Norwegian cream 103–4
Nuts, to store 2–3

Omelettes, soufflé 69–70
Open apricot tart 20–1
Orange cheesecake, cold 75–6
Orange chocolate chip ice cream 148
Orange sorbet 157

Orange soufflé, hot 61
Oranges, caramelized 132–3
Oranges with strawberries 131–2

Pancakes 49–56
  Almond and apricot 51–2
  Apple and cinnamon 51
  Apricot and almond 51
  Bramble and apple 52
  Cinnamon and apple 51
  Classic 50
  Crêpes Suzette 53–4
  French 56
  Saucer pancakes *see* French pancakes
Pancakes, to freeze 47, 49–50
  to reheat 49
Party puddings, cold
  Apricot and lemon mousse 66–7
  Brandy and chocolate layer 109–10
  Chocolate beacon 107–8
  Chocolate and brandy layer 109–10
  Chocolate mousse 113
  Chocolate mousse, rich 67–8
  Chocolate whisky gunge 112
  Coffee walnut layer 111–12
  Crème brûlée 118–19
  French profiteroles 138–9
  Lemon and apricot mousse 66–67
  Lemon cream cheese 114
  Lemon soufflé, sharp 61–2
  Lime mousse, fresh 68–9
  Midnight mousse 65–6
  Old English trifle 115–16
  Pineapple cheesecake mousse 63–4
  Pineapple mousse 62–3
  Profiteroles, French 138–9
  Syllabub 114–15

Party puddings, cold – *continued*
  Walnut coffee layer 111–12
  Whisky chocolate gunge 112
Party puddings, hot
  Apricot brûlée 116–17
  Melon and raspberry brûlée
    117–18
  Soufflês 59–61
Passion pudding 102
Pastry dishes 7–23
  freezing 8
  in larder 6
  puff, bought 137
  refrigerating 8
Pavlova, to freeze 81
Pavlovas 90–3
  Margaret's Pavlova 90–1
  Pavlova with Kiwi fruit 91–2
Peach Melba 150–1
Pears in red wine 133–4
Pie, defined 7
  double crust 7
  freezing 8
  refrigerating 8
Pies 9–10, 10–11, 16–18, 21–2
  Apple 9–10
  Lemon meringue 16–18
  Midsummer fruit 10–11
  Mincemeat and almond 21–2
Pineapple cheese cake mousse 63–4
Pineapple and ginger meringue
  layer 86
Pineapple ice cream 149
Pineapple in Kirsch 131
Pineapple meringue pudding 93–4
Pineapple mousse 62–3
Planning, advance 2
Plum pudding, Christmas 32
Polythene 4
Praline ice cream 151–2
Profiteroles, French 138–9

Queen of puddings 40–1

Radley pudding 30
Raisin, rum and coffee ice cream
  149
Raspberries, freezing 3
  in puddings 121
Raspberry ice cream 149
Raspberry and melon brûlée
  117–18
Raspberry sorbet 157–8
Real thick pouring cream 46
Refrigerating batter 47
  caramel custard 95
  cheesecakes 73
  milk puddings 95
  pastry 8
Rhubarb fool 129–30
Rhubarb and ginger cheesecake
  78–9
Rice pudding, baked 99–100
Rich chocolate mousse 67–8
Rum, coffee and raisin ice cream 149

Saucer pancakes *see* French pan-
  cakes 56
Shortcake, gooseberry 19
Silicone paper 83
Skin, custard, to prevent 97
Sorbets 156–8
  Lemon 156
  Orange 157
  Raspberry 157–8
Soufflé, cold, to freeze 57
  containers 59
  Chilled sharp lemon 61–2
  omelettes 69–70
Soufflés, hot 59–60, 61, 70–1
  Chocolate 59–60
  Coffee 61
  Lemon 60
  Lemon soufflé omelette 70

Lemon soufflé pudding 70–1
 Orange 61
Sponge pudding, steamed 36–7
Sponge puddings 34–7
 Apricot and lemon 37
 Blackcurrant upside down pudding 37–8
 Chocolate 34–5
 Eve's pudding 35–6
 Steamed sponge 36–7
Spotted Dick 33–4
Steamed sponge pudding 36–7
Storing batter, uncooked 47
 containers for 3–4
 cream 3
 in freezer 2–5
 ingredients 2–4
 in larder 5–6
 meringues 81
 nuts 2–3
 pancakes 47, 49–50
Strawberries with oranges 131–2
Strawberries in puddings 121
Strawberry and cream dessert cake 140–1
Strawberry ice cream 149, 152–3
Suet puddings
 Apple and apricot steamed pudding 31
 Apple and blackberry pudding 29
 Blackberry and apple pudding 29
 Christmas plum pudding 32
 Jam roly poly, baked 33
 Jane Grigson's Sussex pond pudding 28–9
 Radley pudding 30
 Spotted Dick 33–4
 Treacle suet pudding 27–8
Sugar, lemon 5
 vanilla 4–5
Summer pudding 126–7

Sussex pond pudding 28–9
Swiss hazelnut meringue with chestnuts 88–9
Syllabub 114–15
Syrup, time-saving 127

Tapioca pudding, baked 100
Tart, defined 7
Tarts 11–14, 18, 20–1, 22–3
 Apricot, open 20–1
 Bakewell 12–13
 English custard 22–3
 Lemon cream 18
 Mincemeat 11–12
 Open apricot 20–1
 Victorian treacle 13–14
Teatime fritters 55
 meringues 81
 pastry treats 7–23
Toffee butterscotch ice cream 148
Traditional winter puddings 25–45
Treacle suet pudding 27–8
Treacle tart, Victorian 13–14
Trifle custard 98
Trifle, old English 115–16
Tutti frutti ice cream 149

Vanilla sugar 4–5
Victorian treacle tart 13–14

Walnut coffee layer 111–12
Whisky chocolate gunge 112
Winter puddings 25–46
 Apple and apricot steamed pudding 31
 Apple and blackberry pudding 29
 Apple with brown sugar crumble 39–40

Winter puddings – *continued*
Apple Charlotte 38–9
Apple dumplings, baked 44
Apricot and apple steamed pudding 31
Apricot and lemon pudding 37
Blackcurrant upside down pudding 37–8
Blackberry and apple pudding 29
Bread and butter pudding 41–2
Bread pudding, Mary Norwak's 42–3
Chocolate pudding 34–5
Christmas plum pudding 32
Eve's pudding 35–6

Jam roly poly, baked 33
Jane Grigson's Sussex pond pudding 28–9
Lemon and apricot pudding 37
Mary Norwak's bread pudding 42–3
Queen of puddings 40–1
Radley pudding 30
Sponge pudding, steamed 36–7
Spotted Dick 33–4
Steamed sponge pudding 36–7
Treacle suet pudding 27–8

Yogurt, home made 101
Apricot yogurt fool 101
Passion pudding 102